Passing the Colors

Engaging Visual Culture in the 21st Century

Chris Stoffel Overvoorde

Passing

the Colors

Engaging Visual Culture in the 21st Century

Chris Stoffel Overvoorde

WILLIAM B. EERDMANS PUBLISHING COMPANY

Grand Rapids, Michigan / Cambridge, U.K.

© 2002 Wm. B. Eerdmans Publishing Co.

Wm. B. Eerdmans Publishing Co.
255 Jefferson Ave. S.E., Grand Rapids, Michigan 49503 /
P.O. Box 163, Cambridge CB3 9PU U.K.

Printed in the United States of America

06   05   04   03   02   01   7   6   5   4   3   2   1

Library of Congress Cataloging-in-Publication Data
ISBN   0-8028-3953-3

This book has been composed in Monotype Haarlemmer

www.eerdmans.com

Contents

Acknowledgments

Writing a book like this cannot be undertaken without the help of many individuals. I look back on more than thirty years of experience with students, fellow faculty members, and the administration at Calvin College, and they include many who deserve special mention.

When I came to the Art Department of Calvin in 1966, I joined three others: the chairman, Edgar Boevé, who as an artist and art historian guided all of us with humor and sensitive insight; Robin Jensen, whose enthusiasm and commitment have been a constant inspiration; and one part-time faculty, Eunice Bolt, who was a marvelous artist-teacher and therefore a good example for me. All of us were searching for new answers, and many of us were involved in several exhibitions, especially the Annual Christian Art Show in Sparta, Michigan.

Carl J. Huisman and Helen Bonzelaar came in 1967. Carl has been a good friend and critic to me over all these years, and his personal interest has inspired me on many occasions. Helen Bonzelaar taught art education, and her enthusiasm and "champagne" character made teaching a joy for me. Later we were joined by the younger generation, like Tim Van Laar, who had studied with me, as did Jim Kuiper. Both of them challenged me to return to painting and printmaking, which I did after a period of administrative commitments. In those days we enjoyed fresh insights and a new sense of community. Ron Peterson, who came to us from Messiah College, invited dialogue, and for some time we freely exchanged ideas and critiqued each other's works.

The need for additional art historians brought us a number of individuals: Brenda Van Halsema, Marilyn Borst, and Virginia Bullock, who later became the Director of Exhibitions. Each of them added to my understanding of art and art history.

Before Ed Boevé retired, Charles Young joined us as an art historian, and his insights have added much to the dialogue within the department. Anna Greydanus Probes joined us later, and we have all benefited from her caring and sharing attitude. Frank Speyers has become special to me, for like myself, Frank came from the graphics industry. His sense of design and understanding of concept is of excellent quality, and I have enjoyed his special challenges over the years.

After Boevé retired, Henry Luttikhuizen joined us. His specialty was Dutch art, and the two of us have talked about Dutch art on many occasions. He is one of the reasons I am now a volunteer at the Art Museum. The most recent person to join the Art Department was Conrad Bakker, who is now occupying my studio at Calvin College. Conrad has already contributed extensively to the Art Department since my departure.

Working with faculty members is not exactly like working with family, but it does shape and hone your ideas and concepts, for they encourage, challenge, and mold you in ways you did not anticipate. The same is true for the many students who were enrolled in my courses. When you are working in a studio setting, the personal interaction with your students is individual and private in many instances. In class critiques, the exchange of ideas and images was often intense. Such dialogue has helped me personally a great deal and is one of the reasons I wanted to write all this down.

Beyond the Art Department, I have worked with many other individuals who supported and challenged me in ways they will never know. Working with Michael Van Denend on the *Spark* magazine has been a joy, and I cannot begin to express my thanks to him for his many acts of kindness and encouragement. Mike has become a special friend in the process. Many others too numerous to list have worked with me on projects that served the college — projects like the Baroque Year, the Multicultural Year, and the Dorm Painting Project.

Writing a book means that you invite responses, and I want to thank Michael Markwick for his comments and insights, as well as my colleagues Carl J. Huisman and Frank Speyers. One person in particular deserves special note: Henry Baron. Becoming an editor for an artist is a daring undertaking, but Henry has been up to it in ways that I respect and value. His sensitivity to my initial utterings has been much appreciated. Thank you, Henry.

And, of course, my actual family has shown much patience and provided significant support. My wife has read all the initial drafts and knows how this book emerged from the foggy recesses of my artistic brain. I owe her my profound gratitude.

This lucid and eloquent essay is the story of a life in art. More specifically, it's the story of a life in visual art — told by the one who lived that life, Chris Stoffel Overvoorde. Chris knows a lot about aesthetics and art theory; he's a theoretically reflective and self-aware artist. That will be evident to the reader. But it's the book of an artist, not of a theoretician. It talks about art from the artist's point of view. And it does so specifically and concretely. Chris talks about his art, in the context of telling the story of his life in art.

Given his beginnings, that his would be a life in art was most unlikely. Reared in a working class family near Rotterdam, everything pointed toward his spending his life in the ship building industry. And indeed, he did spend a few of his late teenage years as a diesel mechanic, having learned that in trade school. But it was boring. So he emigrated to the United States. And as the consequence of a number of fortuitous — or better, providential — happenings, and the openness of the U.S. educational system, he eventually found his way to the art school at the University of Michigan, and from there to the art faculty of Calvin College.

The artist who here tells the story of his life in art is a committed and engaged Christian. There's a deep piety, a rich spirituality, that pervades the book. It's not laid on. The voice of the artist and the voice of the Christian are the same voice. The Christian spirituality expressed is that of an artist; the perspective on art expressed is that of a Christian. The two "co-inhere."

It's a spirituality shaped by the biblical stories; that comes to expression especially in Overvoorde's woodcuts, reproductions of some of which accompany the text. At the same time it's a spirituality that shapes his perception of the world, especially of the sky; that comes to expression in those many awesome sky-scapes that he has painted over the years; reproductions of a few of these also accompany the text. The reproductions give almost no sense of the power of these paintings, however. The paintings are huge, so that, standing before them, one feels engulfed; the space of the sky that's painted flows up and over and behind the viewer.

What I find most engaging about this story of the life of a Christian in art is the insatiable habit, here on display, of asking, and struggling to answer, questions. Why is it appropriate for a Christian to spend his life as an artist? In what way, conversely, does Christianity shape the work of an artist? How should a young person gifted at visual art decide between the career of a designer and the career of an artist? What are the different ways in which an artist can serve a community? This is just a sampling — a very small sampling — of the many questions that Chris has asked himself and tried to answer. Lots of people who work in the arts — they're not unique in this regard! — don't really like to ask themselves questions. And of those who do, some prefer just asking the questions. What makes this book unique is that it's the life story of someone with an artist's eye and hand, a Christian's way of being in the world, and an inquiring mind.

Nicholas Wolterstorff

Chapter One

Introduction

He presented the life of an artist as one of continuing development and challenges.

Virginia Bullock, in "Diversity"

Reasons for Writing

My reasons for wanting to sit down and write this book are numerous; it is hard to list them all. The initial reason was my retirement from Calvin College. The retirement celebration was a time of reflection for others and myself. Virginia Bullock, the Center Art Gallery Director of Exhibitions, wrote a special booklet, "Diversity," in connection with an exhibition of selected alumni students' work. In this booklet she reviewed the various contributions I have made as an artist, teacher, member of various civic and cultural communities, and church member. Reading this booklet made me reflect on the many things I have been involved in, and made me thankful for the gifts and opportunities I have been given. My retirement, in the spring of 1997, was a memorable and humbling experience for me. I have since had to look for other things to occupy my hands and my mind.

A second reason is that I have learned many things during those years, and this is a good time to share some of them. Sharing is a way of testifying about what God has done in your life and recognizing that he has had his way with you all along. As an artist I have learned from my teachers, students, colleagues, neighbors, fellow church members, and fellow artists, as well as from gallery directors and other community leaders.

Another important reason for writing this book is that, in the past few months, several of my former students have called me for direction and support. They are struggling with the same questions I was struggling with some forty years ago when I was considering art as a career. Relating some of my struggles and the understanding I have gained may indeed help others. Writing this book is a way of sharing what I have learned on my journey as a Christian artist.

Becoming an Artist

My initial journey began in a Christian school in Kralingsche Veer, near Rotterdam, the Netherlands, where art was a once-a-week experience — copying a reproduction for one hour late on Friday afternoon, when everyone's mind was on going home. Grade school was followed by a Christian trade school, which was to prepare me to become a shipyard metal worker. Here I received my initial freehand drawing lessons, that is, drawing without a ruler or straight edge. Next were evening classes and a national exam to become a diesel mechanic. I joined a repair crew to work on the ocean liners in the Rotterdam harbor and in the engine hall of the shipyard. It was during my tour of duty in the Dutch Army in the Corps of Engineers that I first experienced what it might be like to be an artist. I became the company artist, drawing military cartoons, making mechanical drawings and drawings for maneuvers, and painting emblems for company events. After my army service, I went back to the shipyard and again worked as a diesel mechanic.

Becoming an artist was not easy for me; it was like traveling a winding road, with many detours. The journey would take me away from the small village of Kralingsche Veer to another continent where I had to learn

Self, *1966, drypoint on aluminum plate, 22″ × 30″*

another language and discover another culture. I emigrated in 1957. During my first years as an immigrant, I worked as a tool and die maker. Two years after my arrival, in 1959, I enrolled as a student at Kendall School of Design in Grand Rapids, Michigan. I graduated in 1961 and began working as a commercial artist. In 1963 I returned to school and enrolled at the University of Michigan, where in 1964 I earned a Bachelor of Science degree in design and in 1966 a Master of Fine Arts degree. That same year I was appointed to teach at Calvin College.

As an artist, I have studied quite a variety of things, ranging from rocks to skies, from prophets to doctrines; and I have explored many different media, ranging from white ground etching to oil painting, from egg tempera to pencil drawing. I have remained active over the years both as a visual designer and as a fine artist. In the end, each one of these experiences has contributed to my education: from metal worker, diesel mechanic, tool and die maker, commercial artist, to fine artist.

Writing as an Artist

I am also motived by the challenge of writing about art as a Christian. Few Christian artists have written extensively about the making of art. There are some books with statements from artists on how they work and what they believe. Such statements often provide insight into what they are doing at the moment or what they are concerned about at this stage in their career. Seldom, if ever, do we find anything beyond such limited verbal expressions. Each art faculty exhibition at Calvin College, for example, was accompanied by statements from us about our work, but we never wrote about the process. Occasionally in class I would talk about the process, especially when I was attempting to motivate students to produce something — something that would interest them, an idea they wished to explore, or a concept they wished to research or study to put in visual form. Teaching students to do something original is not easy, for it requires more than demonstration, more than showing them a technique, a way of

Smoke, Wind, Water,
That Is Rotterdam, *1954,*
black and white tempera
painting, signed C. Stoffel

doing, a way of working. Art students have unique ways of approaching a problem; in order to produce a visual work, they gather information and digest knowledge differently. The artist deals with visual stuff, while the writer deals with verbal material. The current debate on visual rhetoric is important in providing insight into how a work of art gains meaning. It does not help the painter much, however, in creating an image, any image, when he or she is in the privacy of his or her studio and confronted by that big white surface.

Since I began teaching at Calvin in 1966, there have been several important publications related to art by Christian philosophers and theologians, including Calvin Seerveld and Nicholas Wolterstorff. These publications have provided significant insight into how we should view the work of the artist and how the work is used and abused by us. These writers could not, however, approach the subject from an artist's point of view and therefore did not explore the mind of the artist or how the artist gains legitimate

Working on a 66″× 84″ canvas later called Lake Effect *in the studio in 1985 at Calvin College*

insight when he or she is involved in the process of making. It is my intention to provide some understanding of the mind of the artist and discuss the artistic process from a Christian artist's point of view. I recognize that this will still be only one perspective, one point of view, and that everything I say here will necessarily reflect my own style of learning and my own way of working.

My ideas and opinions have been shaped by my personal experiences and my reflections on these experiences. For example, many people have immigrated to the United States, but each one of us has responded differently to the traumatic experience of being transplanted and grafted into another culture. The recognition that my hometown is Kralingsche Veer, and that I will always be a Dutchman who became an American, is an important part of how I see the world. Today I recognize that my interest in space and atmosphere and light, for example, is part of my heritage, training, and education. I see the sky with Dutch eyes, because those are the only eyes I was given. They are in some sense my mother's eyes, for she too was always looking up. All of us need to recognize that what we see, and how we see, is uniquely ours. My love for printmaking, where wood and metal are manipulated in numerous ways to achieve an image, is directly related to my early training as a metal worker in a Rotterdam trade school.

This book, however, is also written because I believe that what I have learned can be of value not only to you, the young artist, but also to your family and friends. I want to appeal to young Christian artists and to emphasize your need to function within a community. Too often you have been merely allowed, instead of accepted; ignored, instead of enabled; ridiculed, instead of honored for your unique insight, painful or joyful or otherwise. What should be your expectation as a young artist? What will you be able to count on when living among us? In sharing something of my journey, I hope to provide guidance, understanding, and encouragement to both the artist and the community.

Top Wave, 1965, acrylic on paper, 30″ × 22″, done while studying with Allen Mullen (Collection of Rev. Richard Duifhuis)

Chapter Two

My Initial Journey

"Come and see."

John 1:46

The Early Years

I was born in the small town of Capelle aan de IJssel, which is about four
miles east of the harbor city of Rotterdam, the Netherlands. The river IJssel
and its dikes provided my playground when I was a youngster. Here I had
a place to play, walk, swim, and dream of faraway places. From the top of
the tall dikes I could view the spacious polders, often either enhanced with
wonderful towering clouds or shrouded in a mysterious fog. Such polder
views are etched in my memory. Along the river were also a number of
shipyards. These provided employment for many of the people living in our
small town. The shipyard was the center of our community. I remember, for
example, being dismissed from school whenever a ship would come down
from its building blocks and glide into the river for the first time. Such
happenings were community events that cultivated a sense of pride and
accomplishment. My maternal grandfather, Anthony den Braber, was often
responsible for such an event because he was the foreman of the carpenters

*Kralingsche Veer with the
Christelijke Gereformeerde
Kerk (Christian Reformed
Church)*

Drawing made in 1952 of the shipyard just before the ship Arica *slipped into the water*

Christian Trade School, 1948

in one of the shipyards. He would build and grease the skids on which these large ships would glide into the water after being named and baptized. (See drawing of *Arica*, 1952, above.) Many of my uncles were either metal workers (Toon and Dirk den Braber) or ship carpenters (Chris and Jan den Braber).

I too wanted to be a carpenter, but for some reason I entered the Christian Trade School, at age 12, as a metal-working student. Elementary school had not been a great experience for me. The only reasonable grades I ever received were in singing and drawing. Drawing sessions were held only once a week, for one hour on Friday afternoon. In many of the grades, drawing sessions consisted of careful copying of reproductions. I remember copying a drawing in grade six of some knot willows. I worked on that particular drawing for several weeks. I also remember making a drawing of the principal while he was telling us something. It was an original drawing of his profile, which emphasized his major features. When he discovered what I was doing, he confiscated it. He had a limited sense of humor. So

Our family in 1942 (left to right: Nel, Anton, Adri, Mom, me, and Dad)

much for encouraging original drawing. I cannot remember hearing about any famous paintings or stories about famous artists while I was in grade school or trade school. The grade school did have many large reproductions of historical paintings on the wall, most of which were done by late-nineteenth-century history painters. Getting good grades in singing or drawing did not mean much in the Calvinistic Christian school I attended. A career in art was not on the list of responsible professions. Moreover, my family belonged to the working class, and that meant that I would attend trade school. Like many of my classmates, I was limited in my choices. Family traditions narrowed the educational choice even more. For me it meant becoming either a metal worker or a carpenter. The class system in our small town was clearly delineated, and it did not exactly encourage the working class to seek higher educational goals.

My dad did not have a trade related to the shipyard industry. He worked in the greenhouses as a vegetable gardener, a job he had started in the summer at age 9. He gave up his gardening job after World War II. During the war he began delivering a weekly paper. After the war, he increased the delivery and collection of moneys for subscriptions to fifteen different daily, weekly, and monthly newspapers and magazines. We all helped him with delivering papers each day, so he became my first boss. Later he worked for the postal service, and after that as a storage clerk in a plumbing supply company. As the oldest boy in a family of seven brothers and two sisters, I learned early in life what responsibility means. In 1944, when I was 9, the Germans picked up my dad during a *razzia* on November 19. While he was gone, a cousin and I took care of his weekly paper routes. My older sister and I helped our mother the best we could during the winter of 1944-45. Food and fuel were precious and often not available toward the end of the war. Dad managed to escape and return home in late January of 1945.

One place where I did receive a good deal of encouragement was the church. This was probably because our family was heavily involved in its various organizations. Mom was involved as a leader in the Ladies' Society. Dad was an elder, chaired the Men's Society, and ran the Boys' Club. Sister Nel was involved with the Young Girls' Association. In the meetings of the Young Men's Society, which later became the Young People's Society, I learned to make public presentations and participate in debates. In our Young Men's Society we selected our own leaders, made up our own agendas, and handled our own programs. The minister or sometimes an elder would attend only at our invitation, and were therefore invited guests only on special occasions. We learned by doing, and as a result I overcame some of my shyness and self-consciousness. I was even elected president of the Young Men's Society at age 20 and later was president of the Young People's Society. It was in those meetings that I initially learned about Abraham Kuyper, D. H. T. Vollenhoven, Herman Dooyeweerd, and Hendrik van Riessen, to name only a few.

In trade school I learned the discipline and craft of working with metal, from smithing to filing, from hand chiseling to metal sheeting. After

Delivering newspapers in 1948

graduating from trade school, I was hired by Piet Smit, one of the large shipyards in Rotterdam. In the shipyard my training continued, and after successfully completing my national exam as a metal worker I was assigned to the engine hall of the shipyard. In the evening I attended night school to prepare for my national exam as a diesel mechanic. When I was sixteen years old, I took the week-long written exam and later faced two days of oral examination in Arnhem. I passed my national examination and received my certificate as a diesel mechanic in 1950. In the shipyard engine hall I eventually became mate to the foreman. Together we would begin the building and construction of an engine, starting with the foundation, using our hands, our tools, and our skills. Later we would complete, with the assistance of many others, the large, forty-five-foot-tall engine. It took about six months to build one of those engines (see photo). For a period of two years I also served on the repair crew, which took me to different parts of the Rotterdam harbor. We worked on board many of the ocean liners of the *Holland-Amerika Lijn.* It was fun to work on these great ships and explore the various spaces and places they contained.

Engine Hall at P. Smit Shipyard, 1956; I was assigned to the top section of the 45-foot-high engine

In 1954 I was called to serve in the Dutch Army. While serving in the Corps of Engineers (Pontoniers), I slowly realized two things. The first was that making cartoons, drawings, and company logos was fun and rewarding. The second was that I was dissatisfied with my career. Toward the end of my army duty I had my own space. Serving as the company artist, I made logos, signs, maps, maneuver plans, and other types of drawings, all of which allowed me to discover what it was like to be an artist. My desire for a change in life intensified because of a renewed relationship with an old neighborhood friend, Herbert Koedoot. Herb had emigrated to the United States with his family and had returned for a visit to the Netherlands to explore his roots. We had many discussions about his new homeland and what it was like to live in America. After Herb returned to the U.S.A., we began to correspond with each other.

When I was discharged from the army in November of 1955, I was dissatisfied with many things — my work, my life, and my status. After six months or so, I quit the shipyard and began working for a smaller engine company, Olthoff Motoren, where they repaired smaller ships. I was a mechanic now, but I was still dissatisfied. Would a career in art be a possibility? When I explored it, I discovered that the Fine Arts Academy in Rotterdam was not an option. I did not have the academic qualifications. It was too late; I was too old and, I began to think, too dumb. The correspondence between Herb Koedoot and me eventually led to my emigration from the Netherlands to the United States. Herb found work for me in Grand Rapids, Michigan, and talked Fred Kramer into becoming my sponsor. Without these two things, immigration to the U.S.A. would have been impossible.

Before my departure in 1957

The Immigration

It is not clear to me why I felt compelled to leave my homeland, my family, and my friends. It was not an easy thing to do. At the time I said that I needed to try it and that if I did not like it, I would come back within two years. Was it simply my need for adventure? In retrospect, it may have been my secret desire to become an artist, but that notion is informed by what happened, not by what I expected.

On Monday, June 17, 1957, I left the port of Rotterdam on the ocean liner *Johan van Oldenbarnevelt* (see photo). The departure was marked by a mixture of deep emotions — a great sense of loss at leaving home and family, and the anticipation of a great adventure. The SS *Johan van Oldenbarnevelt* was not full: only 235 passengers were on board when it sailed from Rotterdam to New York. On its return journey it would transport 2,500 students. (I still have the passenger list and some menu cards.)

Because of the small number, everyone was treated royally as first-class passengers. It was a pleasant voyage across the Atlantic Ocean, with no storms or discomforts of any kind.

After ten days of ocean, we saw land on the horizon. It was exciting, and I was filled with anticipation as well as apprehension when the skyline of New York City came into view. Very early the next morning we entered the harbor, and I could see the Statue of Liberty shimmering in the early morning sunlight. By late morning we disembarked, cleared customs, and then I found my way to the bus station on Forty-fourth Street.

The SS Johan van Olden-barnevelt

My first impressions were highly memorable. Standing in line to get my tickets, I confronted my first challenge. The language was a major obstacle because my vocabulary was extremely limited. I knew about twenty-five

Arriving in the harbor of New York City on board the S.S. Johan van Oldenbarnevelt, *1957*

words in English. There was an early bus, but I was made to understand that I should take the next one, for it would not stop as often. I agreed to wait and checked in my suitcases. Everything I owned was in these suitcases. It would be a long wait, so I left the station and took a walk in the immediate neighborhood. Outside, it was 98 degrees, and I was still wearing wool pants, a long-sleeved shirt, and a wool jacket. The first sights were overwhelming; it was all too big, too strange, and too incomprehensible for me. I was actually walking around in New York City. There were people everywhere. In the window of a restaurant I saw an advertisement for Heineken Beer. It reminded me of home, and so I went inside and had a cool beer. It tasted delightful and refreshing. When I returned to the station in time to take the next bus, I looked for my suitcases. They were nowhere to be found, and no one seemed to know what had happened to them. Fortunately, I had kept my papers and my tickets with me, so I was not stranded. But with a heavy heart I boarded the bus. My limited vocabulary did not allow me to understand what had happened. The bus trip to Detroit took almost twenty-four hours. The bus did stop several times to allow the passengers to get something to eat and use the bathroom. My limited vocabulary included such words as "hot dog" and "Coca Cola," so I was able to get some food during those stops. Still, it was a long trip for me.

When the bus arrived in Detroit, it was time to get off and meet my friend Herb Koedoot. Herb was enrolled as a student at a barber college in downtown Detroit. After getting off the bus, I looked for him. He was not there. I waited, but he did not come. He had sent me the address of the school and had told me that it was close to the bus station. In desperation, I left the station and managed somehow to get to the school. When I entered the place, they wanted to put me in a chair. The students gained experience by cutting the hair of the homeless, and after riding that bus day and night, dressed in well-worn wool, I must have looked like a good candidate. When I mentioned Herb's name I got a very different response. The right connection was soon made. The two of us met again, much to my delight. I told him what had happened. He took me to his place, and there I was able to take my first hot/cold American shower. What a pleasure and what a strange experience. Back home we had only one faucet in the house for the whole family of twelve. Here they had hot and cold water in several rooms. Herb got me some fresh clothes to wear, for I still did not know where my suitcases were. The next day he put me on the bus to Grand Rapids, where I arrived late in the afternoon on June 29, 1957. His brother Gerrit, who had been in many of my grade school classes, picked me up. To my delight and relief, we discovered the suitcases in the baggage room. They had come with the earlier bus.

New Challenges

The early years in America were hard for me because I had to face many things alone. My maternal grandfather and one of my favorite uncles died within the first nine months of my arrival here. I did not find out about it till weeks had passed, long after they were buried. I felt alone in this strange new place, for it was not easy to master the language and gain a deeper understanding of the American culture. But when I think back now, I also recognize that in that loneliness and in these struggles I grew closer to God. I began to realize his leading in my life more acutely. God wanted me to be here, and he would see me through all this.

My first job was a fiasco. Eight days after my arrival, I was hired by Lear Siegler as a first-class lathe operator. I began work on Wednesday, July 10, 1957. Because of the language, it was difficult and challenging. I could, however, read the blueprints, and that was enough to know what was needed. My old training paid off. After a couple of weeks, the foreman informed me that I was being assigned to the night shift. At noon that day, the union steward began talking with me about joining the union. I was open, honest, and rather naïve. In the Netherlands I had belonged vol-untarily to a Christian Trade Union (CVN). But things were different here.

From my perspective, joining the union here was not a voluntary action. Even with my limited vocabulary, I raised questions, apparently too many of them. We talked about choice and freedom. Two days later I was out on the street, confused and bewildered by the American idea of choice and freedom. I learned something from that. Freedom here comes in packages; some you can open, and others you must not touch.

The following Monday I began a new job as a tool and die maker in the tool room at Keeler Brass, a haven for many of the newly arrived Hollanders. It was a hot job and a noisy environment in the screw plant on Stevens Street. I made screw dies and fixed the machines from 3:00 till 11:30 p.m., and sometimes later. It was not the best job, but it was good to have one. With one of my first paychecks I bought a bike and began to explore the town.

*With Warren Van Ess
playing chess, 1958*

One of the first places I discovered was a store called Dolores Art Supplies. Dolores and her husband, Lee Powers, ran the place, and they made me feel welcome. Dolores occasionally taught country painting in the back of the store. In the front of the store were displays of local artists' work, which included the work of Warren Van Ess. Warren had done some interesting pen drawings. I liked doing pen drawings myself, and at the urging of Lee and Dolores I called Warren and visited him. He became my first American friend. Warren was a polio victim who painted and drew with a brush in his mouth. He was paralyzed from the neck down and had limited use even of his neck. We talked, critiqued each other's work, and drew together. We also played chess and checkers. We supported each other as friends, and I visited him for many years. He was in many ways an inspiration to me. But my secret dream to become some kind of artist was still only a dream.

How could I make that dream become reality? How could I become an artist? That was the question that haunted me. It seemed to me, as to many Christian Reformed young people at the time, that the only responsible way to do this would be to become a graphic artist. Somehow the notion of becoming a fine artist was too wild, too bohemian, too crazy to contemplate seriously. My Calvinistic upbringing demanded a greater sense of responsibility toward work and security. Obviously, my notions about art were hazy, if not confused, in those days.

At first I tried a correspondence course in an attempt to become a commercial artist, but after three lessons I dropped that idea. I was still not sure how to pursue an educational route that would fulfill my dreams. During that time the members of the Young People's Society at Sherman Street Christian Reformed Church were patient, kind, and supportive. I also developed some friendships with Dutch and Canadian Calvin College students, who encouraged me in many ways to return to school. At the end of January 1959, I applied at Kendall School of Design. One thing that was required, but I did not have, was a high school diploma. I did have all sorts of certificates and diplomas from the various trade schools and evening schools I had attended in the Netherlands. That was enough to get me accepted without conditions. To my amazement I was admitted immediately, in spite of the fact that the semester was three weeks under way.

With Greta Duifhuis in Wyoming, Ontario, where she was a teacher

So on February 2, 1959, I went back to school, on my way at last toward obtaining my goal and realizing my dream. For the next two years I attended class from 8:30 a.m. to 4:30 p.m. and worked at Keeler Brass from 5:00 p.m. to 12:30 a.m., or even later. After that I went home and did my homework. On Thursday nights I took off from work so that I could attend the meetings and drawing sessions of the Grand Valley Artists Association (GVA). That was my only social contact during those years. This group of realistic, naturalistic artists was very supportive of my work.

The public debate about abstract and realistic art was heated in those days in the public press. Three teachers from the University of Michigan Extension Program were proponents of modern art; the members of GVA defended realism and naturalism. I did not have time in my busy schedule or much inclination to participate in the debate. I was still a student and in the process of becoming an artist. Kendall School was a traditional place where drawing was essential. Life drawing was exploratory, experimental as well as realistic. The same was true for the watercolor classes. Courses in design, advertising layout, and typography were also traditional and practical. My basic training here was the mastering of skills. Realism and naturalism were an integral part of my program of study as a visual designer.

The Kendall School curriculum emphasized the doing of art as a way of learning. More than 80 percent of the program was studio work, and I enjoyed every minute of it. It was a practical program that emphasized the various tasks of a visual designer, reflecting the demands of the job market. The visual design program included television art, television programming, and television planning and production. As a student I became involved in several live productions called *College Omnibus* on the local television station, WOOD TV. I was a participant, producer, or director in these thirty-minute-long, live productions.

My drawing instructor, Reynold Weidenaar, introduced me to printmaking in his home studio as well as to watercolor painting in class. Weidenaar was a Christian Reformed artist. He was an elder in the church and active as an artist in the community. How these two activities were related to each other he never discussed with me, even in private. I respected him, however, a great deal. Reynold was what art historians call a regionalist, recording and responding to the local scenery and events. His Christian commitment was expressed neither in the classroom at Kendall School nor at his numerous exhibitions.

I continued to study at Kendall School of Design in the summer months and was thus able to complete the three-year program in two years.

New Opportunities

At the end of January 1961, I was laid off from my job at Keeler Brass. I was behind in my school tuition and my room and board payments. When I went to the director of Kendall to discuss the situation with him, he contacted Steketee Van Huis for me. After a good interview with the staff there, I was hired on the spot. On February 1, 1961, I began my career as a visual designer at Steketee Van Huis Printing in Holland, Michigan. I had escaped the factory and was on my way toward a new life. It was a good job for a beginning visual designer, because the same art department, consisting of three people, served the Steketee Van Huis Printing Company, the Adex Advertising Agency, and later the Holland Packaging Corporation. The printing plant used mostly offset printing, with some letterpress printing. Typesetting was done by hand, using Linotype machines and letterboxes, some of which still included wooden letters. The advertising agency created all sorts of advertisements for professional journals as well as brochures and other promotional materials. The packaging corporation allowed us to create things that were three-dimensional, and designing packages became a special challenge for us. In the beginning I commuted between Grand Rapids and Holland, but after six months I moved to Holland to be closer to the job. I rented the upstairs of a house, which provided both a studio space and a good living space.

In July 1962, on Friday the thirteenth, I married Greta Duifhuis. She had emigrated to Canada at the age of 16 with her family. She had attended the Reformed Bible College in Grand Rapids, and later Calvin College, from which she graduated in 1963. When we were courting in 1961, she was working in Wyoming, Ontario, teaching grades five through eight in the Christian school. Marrying Greta was the best thing that ever happened to me, for she became not only my greatest critic but also my biggest supporter.

After graduating from Kendall School of Design, I continued my education by attending evening classes at Grand Rapids Junior College, where I enrolled in my first English grammar course. I had learned the language by listening and by trying to speak; according to Greta, it was time to gain a better understanding of the structure of the language. Later I also took some writing courses. In Holland I also continued my art training through private lessons with Harry Brorby, who had studied printmaking with Maurice Lasinsky at the University of Iowa. Harry in his soft-spoken manner introduced me to intaglio printmaking, a process that fascinated me. Reynold

On our wedding day, July 13, 1962, in the Calvin Seminary Chapel

Weidenaar, my teacher at Kendall, was a well-known printmaker. He had shown me his plates and his tools in his studio, but he would not take me on as a private student or assistant. Harry Brorby opened my eyes to the many image-making possibilities in both printmaking and painting. In printmaking he emphasized the exploratory approach, in which the printmaker "bites" the plate with acids, then, after reviewing the results, modifies the image by scraping and burnishing the copper plate. This was the approach Harry had learned from Lasinsky at the University of Iowa. You could work on a plate for many weeks, slowly searching for a final image. In painting he suggested a greater involvement with the process. Brorby taught us that the act of painting was a way of finding and clarifying an image. Up to now I had started with an image in my mind first, so this was a radically different approach for me. Harry was not only my teacher; he also became a friend and advisor.

After a year of studying with him, he made it clear that I should continue my education, an idea that Greta supported completely. A friend of mine asked Harry what he thought of me as an artist, to which Harry replied: "Chris cannot live without art." He sensed my commitment, my conviction that I should be an artist, and he realized that the day-to-day monotony of being a graphic artist was not enough for me. Key-line and paste-up could be challenging in some ways, but they could also be repetitive and dull. In those days such work was all done by hand on an actual paste-up board, gluing in each section, sometimes even individual letters, with rubber cement. It was a tedious process. The graphic arts industry has of course seen major changes; today all of this is done much more simply and quickly on a computer.

Brorby sent me to the University of Michigan with a recommendation. The chair of the School of Art, Robert Iglehart, interviewed me. He examined my work, looked at my academic credits, and to my surprise immediately admitted me to the art program. In the fall of 1963 we moved to Ann Arbor so that I could attend the University of Michigan. Greta found a job teaching in the South Salem Stone School, a one-room country school just north of Ann Arbor near Northville. She taught twenty-eight students from kindergarten to grade six. By now I was no longer the shy, quiet person who had left the Netherlands. My doubts about becoming an artist were fading fast. The possibility of my dream becoming a reality was right in front of me. But it was not easy to return to school.

At first I was in a daze. It was all hard to believe. Many times I was afraid, and I felt lost among the 40,000 students attending the University of Michigan. But I soon gained confidence, especially after receiving a bit of praise. The experience of university life allowed me to break out of my Dutch-ghetto mentality. Being a Dutchman in Ann Arbor was not like being one in Grand Rapids. The Dutch heritage, still largely unknown to myself, was respected and honored by my university professors and my fellow graduate students. I especially developed a meaningful relationship with some of the graduate students in the Art History Department. My ignorance of my own heritage was embarrassing. Before leaving the Netherlands in 1957, I had visited only one art museum: a year before I left, I saw a large retrospective exhibition of the works of Rembrandt van Rijn at the Museum Boymans van Beuningen. *The Anatomy Lesson of Dr. Tulp,* which was part of this exhibit, made a lasting impression on me. This one-time visit, however, was an isolated event for me. Many immigrants, including myself, were culturally deprived and uninformed about their rich Dutch cultural heritage when they left the Netherlands. When I reflect on my earlier education, I am acutely aware of the fact that art was not a part of it in any form. My Christian grade school teachers most likely had a negative view of art or a misguided conception of what art was. Their religious views may have blinded them to how important art had been historically and culturally to the Netherlands. At the University of Michigan I heard people speak highly about Dutch artists. This was especially true in Dr. Wolfgang Stechow's class on the history of northern painting. Stechow was an inspiration to me. He spoke to me in a kindly way after

In the print studio at the University of Michigan, 1964

Trees, *1964, watercolor,*
12″ × 14″

class, and allowed me to write my final exam for his class in Dutch. The new perspective and insights made the integration into the American culture easier for me. It also gave a boost to my self-confidence as an art student and as a person.

Learning and Discovering

My career also began to move along a smoother path. Initially, I was enrolled as a graphic art student. I wanted to earn my Master's in visual design. But soon after I began my studies, it became clear that I wanted to be a printmaker instead. Switching from being an advertising designer to becoming a fine artist was not easy. (I will elaborate more fully on that issue in Chapter 4.) I studied with two printmakers: Frank Cassara (intaglio and silk-screen) and Emile Weddige (lithography and woodcut), and two painters: William Lewis (watercolor) and Allen Mullen (acrylic). All four were very good to me and taught me much about image making and about

Trees in Wind and Rain,
1965, watercolor, 22″ × 30″,
done while studying with
William Lewis

Blue Wave with Red, *1965,*
acrylic on paper, 22″ × 32″,
done while studying with
Allen Mullen

myself. Their honesty and openness allowed me to grow and mature as an artist. All of them instilled in me a sense of the discipline of art, as well as a need to explore.

In the mid-1960s it was popular to explore *ARTNews,* for it was the magazine that set the trends for the rest of the art world. Pop Art and Op Art were in, and anything else was out. Robert Hughes in his book *Nothing If Not Critical* describes how the Australian artists responded:

> The copy of *ARTNews* would arrive and we would dissect it, cutting out the black-and-white reproductions and pinning them on the studio wall. . . . This act of unwonted humility was made by thousands of people concerned with making, distribution, teaching and judgement of art, not only in places like Australia but throughout Europe and — not incidentally — America in the mid-1960's. (6-7)

And so it was in graduate school at the University of Michigan in Ann Arbor. I was not interested, however, in either Op Art or Pop Art. Nor did I want to take my inspiration from the latest in *ARTNews.* I was interested in landscape painting, especially trees. Moreover, I was more motivated to do watercolors than oils. When I approached Professor Lewis about doing a series of watercolors on trees, he was somewhat shocked, which, given the cultural climate at the time, was understandable. His initial response was vague and noncommittal. But he did not stop me. I knew that if I wanted to do trees, I should become familiar with trees. I knew that the best way to do this was to draw them. I didn't need a lot of biological detail about trees, nor did I need to be able to tell what kind of tree I was looking at, although that would be helpful at times. No, I needed to look, to study the visual appearance of trees with a fresh mind and an open eye. I began by making sketches and final drawings of trees out in the countryside. In other words, I returned to nature for information and inspiration. I had to make my own personal commitment to do so and pursue in my own way the things that were or could become important to me. I needed to set aside what was popular in New York, or anywhere else for that matter.

After a few weeks of making drawings of trees, my renderings became looser and freer. I switched to watercolor, and the use of brushes allowed me to be even more spontaneous. This direction may have been influenced by the courses I was taking on the history of Chinese painting. I admired the individual brush marks of the Chinese painters and their personal manner of composing an image. Buddhist Chinese painters get into a high state of Zen tranquility and perfected consciousness before they paint. With quick and masterful spontaneous brush strokes, they produce remarkable images, free and loose, yet supremely controlled. In my own studio space, I found myself mentally preparing, setting out paints and brushes, establishing a place for each item needed in the painting process before I began to paint. I would often work in total quietness, without the sound of radio or tape player invading my space.

When I was convinced that this was the right direction for me, I was ready for my first critique with Professor Lewis. After he had seen the results of my approach and how I was employing the medium, he became interested. From that first critique on, he advised me a great deal. I later learned that he himself was an excellent watercolorist, so he knew from personal experience the power and the possibilities of this unique medium. I was a rather traditional watercolorist who used only washes and brushes to establish an image. Lewis challenged me to broaden my view and to add other tools such as pencils, pens, and markers to the washes and the brush strokes. Due to his encouragement, the mark-making became more and more important to me. The first semester of studying under Lewis, I completed about seventy watercolors on paper on the subject of trees. Our weekly coffee breaks became significant moments. I remember a particular critique with him when I was in my second year. I had switched to acrylic painting at the urging of Allen Mullen. Lewis and I were discussing a major work on canvas. It was four feet by eleven feet in size. I called it *John the*

White Wave, *1965, acrylic on paper, 22″ × 30″, done while studying with Allen Mullen*

Baptist. The canvas was too large to be critiqued in the studio, so we moved it into the staircase of the building. During coffee break I had related to him, rather enthusiastically, how I saw John the Baptist's cry in the wilderness. When he saw the work, he took his time responding. When he finally spoke, he said this: "What you said in the coffee shop is different from what you are doing here." It took me a while to accept that, for it had not yet dawned on me that what we think we see is not always what we really see. The mind can play tricks on us, because what we believe modifies what we see and how we see it. I needed to learn that what we desire is not always what we make; what we think we see and believe is therefore seldom clear to others. Communication is a fickle thing, I discovered. Bill Lewis was kind, supportive, and interested in spending time with me. He was also open, honest, and direct when he spoke to me. He did not play games. He inspired me to grow and produce good works.

Professor Frank Cassara, the intaglio printmaker instructor, was another inspiration for me. He was soft-spoken, but his personal critiques were challenging and thought provoking. He was always questioning the composition and its relationship to the content. He often discussed how it worked and why, for he was sensitive to the image as a whole and to the different levels of meaning that were implied. Frank Cassara taught me to see the structure of a work more clearly than any previous instructor. His prodding made me understand that the black and white organization of a work is essential to its success. His formal approach required me to re-examine my understanding of how art functions. As a visual designer you follow what works; you use established ways and means to get the message across by combining words and image in a unique way. It is a kind of puzzle. When you can make the pieces of the puzzle fit, you have an image. The drudgery of everyday production schedules, however, leaves little room for exploration. There is not much creativity in doing key-line and paste-up all day. I needed to learn more about the mysteries of creating visual images if I was going to be a fine artist. I needed to explore more freely and search more deeply. The question for me was, can one communicate visually without a story? Can art function without content? I found it hard to let go of the obvious answers and become a playful Calvinist. My rigid theoretical, doctrinal approach to creativity was limiting me. Yet I was not ready to jump with both feet into an abyss of exploration and experimentation without meaning. Nancy Chinn, in her book *Spaces for Spirit: Adorning the Church*, writes:

> The need for visual illustration has been met with pictures made by skillful hands, pictures that breathe as art. Contrast, for example, one of Da Vinci's Madonnas and a Christmas card from the stack sent and received each year. What is the difference? Both formats are narrative; both tell the story. Both are perhaps romantic, depicting an ideal, a vision of mother and child a bit removed from the actual reality of childbirth, nursing and rearing. But the difference is that one evokes a sense of mystery and the other seems silly. One seems awesome, the other only trite. One speaks of cosmos, of sacred timelessness; the other of the mere present. In the Da Vinci Madonna, the viewer is invited by aesthetic skill to let God interrupt all assumptions. The greeting card offers a predictable and easy answer to life's complexities. (4-5)

At one of the outdoor shows in 1964

My weekly meetings with Cassara slowly helped me explore new ways of finding the mystery in things visual. From the very first semester, when he hired me to be his assistant, to the last semester, when I taught printmaking for him as a teaching assistant, he was my mentor and my guide. Later, as a drawing teacher, I would challenge my advanced students to make drawings that did not have any story, setup, or object in them. The basic question was, can art communicate when we have no story, no subject, that is, no obvious connections? Can we make marks in different ways, and when we do, are the marks communicating different perceptions and meaning? These students would just make marks and thereby learn that the *way* the marks were made, and *where* the marks were made, became the content of the work. They learned about the notion of subject and content: that the way you portray a given subject becomes the content.

A subject can have many aspects, and what we choose to say about a subject is a complex issue. How we choose to say it is also complex. Learning *how* to speak visually is as important as *what* we have to say. Mark-making is at the heart of visual communication. Nothing is more personal than your intentional mark. It is like your signature, uniquely yours. The mark-making search may allow you to discover the mystery of making meaningful images — images that are curious; images that invite further questions; images that affirm, confess, and challenge what we already know.

In my printmaking classes I was exploring a number of religious images, such as the woodcut print "Forbid Them Not . . ." and the etching "From Weeping to Fruitbearing." Cassara never questioned the religious nature of these images; on the contrary, he was always supportive of the concepts I was working with. But when the review committee of the faculty raised questions about these religious images, I replied: "You wish me to work on images that are important and significant to me? Well, these are the ideas and concepts I care a great deal about, these are the issues that matter to me and that is why I am doing them." After that, I was never questioned or challenged again by the art faculty. I did, however, have some good conversations with my instructors. Time and again, my Dutch Reformed theological mind would run ahead of me and dictate an image, rather than discover the image in the process of doing. My instructors always challenged that approach. They wanted me to learn that the answer was within the image rather than in my mind.

The work I was doing in watercolor became more and more spontaneous. It was through the use of watercolor that I discovered some of the answers I had been looking for. In watercolor I would start with only a general notion about the direction these works were taking. But a general concept was enough to begin my exploration. The particular notion would guide my initial marks, and after that things would just develop. A series of

From Weeping to Fruit-bearing, *1966, hardground etching, 22″ × 32″ 1966, done while studying with Frank Cassara*

Forbid Them Not . . . ,
1966, woodcut, 36″ × 48″,
done while studying with
Emile Weddige

decisions, made while the work was in process, would begin to dictate things. I would add a mark here, a stroke there, a little more water here, until something emerged that I could recognize as a final image. When I was done the results would often surprise me. The process of doing was providing a greater sense of direction than any preconceived ideas I had before I began.

In my etching classes, too, I began to explore more. I reworked the copper and zinc plates again and again, biting, scraping, and scratching the image, making this edge softer, and that shape darker, and that texture richer. I would often work in pencil and charcoal on a proof print to search for a better image. After many stages of reworking, a final image would slowly emerge. This image would be richer and more vibrant than the image I started with. The method was not new to me; it had first been introduced to me by Harry Brorby, who had studied at the University of Iowa print studio where Cassara had also worked for a while. With Cassara's help, I finally began to understand what Harry had been trying to teach me all along.

Allen Mullen challenged me more than the others to play with a new medium, acrylic, which he had discovered as an artist working in New York. Some of us bought the powdered pigments and the medium to create our own paints, while others bought the new plastic tubes made available by only one manufacturer. I used a lot of the commercially available latex paints and mixed them with the new acrylic paints. It was all experimental and playful. This approach allowed me to explore an image in a wholly different manner. It was risky, for you could never be sure when a work was done, or how good it was, until it dried and you put a mat on it. Acrylic paints have a way of drying differently, sometimes lighter, sometimes darker. When you compare watercolor with acrylic, you recognize that watercolor is a transparent medium. Acrylic, on the other hand, is a medium that is both transparent and opaque. Moreover, when you work with watercolor, the paints remain sensitive to water after drying; not so when you work with

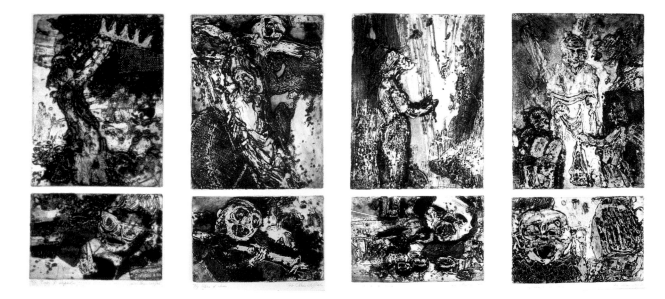

acrylic. Acrylic thus allows you to work in many different kinds of layers, sometimes glazing, sometimes scumbling. Glazing is like applying a transparent color film over a section. Scumbling is when you use an opaque layer over a section, partially blocking out the section. This playful approach allowed me a great deal of freedom to explore.

In the summer of 1965, I produced eighty works on paper combining watercolor and acrylic, working with transparent and opaque passages on the idea of wave movement and the power of water. This broad approach to exploring a theme was helpful to me, because it provided a much-needed respite from the controlled and preconceived ideas I had been working with before. Thinking about an image, projecting in my mind what it would look like, had always come first. But now I would begin with only a notion, and the doing began to provide insights I had not considered before. The process of making art required a continuous series of responses, alternating between doing and thinking, thinking and doing. I tried to apply this

The Virtues and the Vices,
*collagraph prints, each
image 11″ × 23″*

from left to right:
1. *Fides & Superbia
[faith & pride]*
2. *Spes & Ira
[hope & despair]*
3. *Caritas & Gula
[charity & gluttony]*
4. *Justicia & Invidia
[justice & envy]*
5. *Temperantia & Luxuria
[temperance & lust/luxury]*
6. *Fortitudo & Accidia
[courage & sloth]*
7. *Prudentia & Avaricia
[wisdom & avarice]*

playful, exploratory approach to printmaking and eventually succeeded somewhat in liberating myself from the restrictiveness of a preconceived image. Audrey Flack reflects a similar experience in her book *Art and Soul: Notes on Creating:*

> I always wanted to draw realistically. For me, art is a continuous discovery of reality, an exploration of visual data, that has been going on for centuries, each artist contributing to the next generation's advancement. I wanted to go a step further and extend the boundaries. I also believe people have a deep need to understand their world, and that art clarifies reality for them. (19)

In Chapter 3, "The Calling and Task of the Artist," I will return to this topic of learning by doing.

Theories, theologies, concepts, and ideas from the history of art were constantly floating around in my head. In one art history seminar, we studied and discussed the *Psychomachia* — a poem written by Prudentius about the battle between the virtues and the vices. Each student in the class studied a different manifestation of that poem and reported on his or her findings at our weekly seminar meetings. My fellow students were Ph.D. candidates and were well prepared for this sort of approach. I was assigned to make a presentation on the works of Hieronymous Bosch, focusing on the *Tabletop with the Four Last Things and the Seven Deadly Sins.* I enjoyed the class, especially the discussions and the various presentations by the others. My report on Bosch was well received. In Bosch's work, the concepts depicted around the center of the tabletop dealt with the seven deadly sins in everyday situations. In the very center was the resurrected Christ surrounded by the words: "Beware, beware, God is watching." The idea of the seven virtues and vices intrigued me beyond the requirements of the class. I began making drawings to explore the possibilities, because I needed to respond to these ideas with more than words. I wanted to produce my own images of the virtues and vices. Eventually I did so, using a brand new medium. This medium is now called collagraphy — a combination of the words *collage* and *graphics.* This designation did not yet exist when I was doing these prints. Frank Cassara had explored some images using this approach and had shared the results with me. He suggested to me, as his printmaking assistant, that I should try this approach as well. I did several prints before beginning this series on the virtues and vices. These seven prints, made up of fourteen plates and a number of templates, became my major project in the graduate intaglio print classes with Frank Cassara.

Emile Weddige, my lithography professor at the University of Michigan, was a different kind of role model for me. Weddige was an excellent printmaker who emphasized the technique and discipline of lithography in a forceful manner. He was open and honest about what he required, and his approach was very different from that of Frank Cassara. Images were seldom discussed in depth, and we seldom had a class critique or even a personal critique. All he required was a "good" print. He was extremely critical when he was reviewing an edition with you. An edition is a series of prints made from a block, stone, or plate that should be alike. At the end of each semester, all the students enrolled in his classes were required to display their work in a large room. The students would go around that room, look at the works, and make judgments about the success or failure of each print. A vote *for* meant that the student appreciated the work. The votes would be tallied and written on the blackboard by Weddige. Everyone would know the score and would know who was appreciated as a print-maker. On the basis of the total votes you received, Weddige would determine the grade for that semester. It was an ingenious system. Your peers were truly judging you. In a way it was a marvelous community affair, but it was also a kind of popularity contest. My print buddy, Bill Davison, and I were always in the top spot, alternating each semester for the highest honors. Being judged by your peers in this way is an important lesson, because one of the major activities for an artist is successful participation in juried exhibitions. Such exhibitions, which allow you to establish a name for yourself as an artist, are often judged by your peers.

Weddige was responsible for teaching both lithography and relief printing, which includes woodcut printing. But his love was lithography. So you needed to be stubborn and persistent if you wanted to learn about woodcut. On one occasion someone had tried to make a large woodcut, but was unable to complete the image. I requested the use of that block, to which Professor Weddige replied with a grumble: "You want to build a house? You need a big idea for such a big block." In response I returned to my studio space and made a large ink drawing the size of the block. When I was done, I displayed the drawing across from his office. The door was closed. His office door was always closed when he was having lunch, and we did not dare to interrupt him during this time. So I sat down next to the drawing, eagerly awaiting the moment when he would open the door again. After some time he did. He stood in the doorway and stared at the drawing for several minutes, then closed the door again behind him without saying a

In my studio space in Graduate School at the University of Michigan with the drawing and the partially cut block of the woodcut Forbid Them Not . . .

word. He had not even looked at me. What should I do? I waited till he came out again. "Do you know where the woodshop is?" was his only question. He made no comment on the image, not then and not later. But he did give me a work order to have the block planed down. That block became my first large woodcut; I called it "Forbid Them Not . . ." Later I also explored the wood engraving medium by making a number of small images. I wanted to study all the print media so that I could truly call myself a printmaker, rather than a lithographer, an etcher, etc. As a result, I was trained in all the major print media: intaglio and silk-screen with Cassara, and lithography and relief with Weddige.

Building a Support Community

Greta was interested in what I was learning and doing at the university, even though she was very busy teaching twenty-eight students in the one-room South Salem Stone School. Later she taught grade three for the South Lyon Public School. She learned with me in spite of her own job and taught me various ways to study. Greta showed me how to master many of the liberal arts subjects I was taking along with my studio courses. Together we learned about art and art history. We explored the implications of what it meant to be a Christian artist. In those days, material on a Christian approach to art was hard to come by. Helpful books by Calvin Seerveld, Bruce Lockerbie, Hans Rookmaaker, and Nicholas Wolterstorff had not yet been published.

One place where I did receive additional incentive was the Christian Reformed University Chapel. Reverend Donald Postema began his chaplaincy at the same time that we arrived in Ann Arbor. Don and his wife Elaine were interested in and informed about the arts, and we benefited from their support and interest. I served on the steering committee of the University Chapel. It was at the chapel that we met several graduate students who were involved in the fine arts, like Donna Spaan, who was in drama, and William Oldenburg, in creative writing. Their understanding of art and Christianity was helpful to me, and their moral support kept me going.

The Struggle, *1962, oil on panel, 24″ × 24″. Now in the collection of Daniel De Graaf Galleries. This work received first place in the Christian Art Show of 1962.*

As a member of the steering committee, I also became involved with the redecoration of the University Chapel basement. We had little money, so whatever we did had to be done inexpensively. Banners were just beginning to become popular in some denominations. The committee requested that I design a series of banners for the chapel basement. After some discussion, the theme of the seven deadly sins was selected. Greta and others did the sewing of the banners after I did the design. Together we selected the colors and the materials. As a committee member, I also designed a new logo for the chapel and a cover for the weekly worship bulletin. Both are still being used today. These were my first experiences working with a Christian community. It taught me how a Christian artist could be a serving artist within the church. The idea of being a Christian artist was no longer just an abstract dream for me — it was a concrete reality. I found that using my gifts in this way was both exciting and satisfying.

Another place that became important to me, for we learned a great deal about Christian art and Christian artists there, was the Peace Lutheran Church in Sparta, Michigan, which organized the Annual Christian Art Show. Pastor Roy Schroeder and his artist wife, Joy, started this juried exhibition in 1962. It occupied all the available spaces of the church, from sanctuary to Sunday School rooms, during Holy Week. Though it was only one week long, the exhibit became very popular, due in large measure to the promotional skills of the Schroeders. They challenged the entire religious art community in the Grand Rapids area to submit excellent work to the competition. Each year the amount of award money increased, making it more and more appealing to artists to participate. The newspapers and television stations covered the announcements and the event itself. Many of the prize-winning artists appeared on local television talk shows to discuss their work and explain their views. On Easter Sunday there was an hour-long television show, which incorporated many of the works submitted to the juried exhibition. Panel discussions and artist presentations were scheduled by the church into the events of Holy Week.

Jurors spoke about their selection process or published statements about their views. I can especially remember Dr. Piepkorn and Siegfried Reinhardt as excellent speakers.

For me it all began in 1962 with a surprising phone call from Pastor Schroeder. He informed me that two of my works were prize winners: I had been awarded first and fourth place that year. I was surprised because I didn't know that any of my works had actually been entered. An artist friend, Herman Mayer, had suggested the show to me and had asked if he could take some works for me, and I had agreed. He had taken care of the details, and as a result I did not know which works, if any, he had entered. It was a very pleasant surprise to receive these awards. Previously that year I had received an award at the Muskegon Regional Competition at the Hackley Art Gallery. This honor was different, however, because it came from a church, and it was a great boon to me as a fellow believer. I have supported the Annual Christian Art Show ever since and have received many additional awards there. When Roy and Joy Schroeder moved to East Lansing, Michigan, to shepherd the Ascension Lutheran Church there, they eventually took the show with them and continued the effort in East Lansing. From the beginning, these two congregations purchased art from the competition. Each now has a fine collection of paintings, prints, sculptural works, and banners as well as vestments and works on paper. I am pleased to say that I am well represented in the collections of both congregations. (I will elaborate more fully on the importance of exhibitions, competitions, galleries, and museums in Chapter 5, "My Journey as an Artist.")

Looking back on the early part of my journey, I recognize the importance of many individuals in my life. My wife Greta, who learned with me and has remained my constant companion and supporter for more than forty years, has been a major blessing in my life. Harry Brorby's encouragement and direction, particularly in urging me to attend the University of Michigan, was crucial to my career in fine arts. The support of the small group of Christian students at the University Chapel was of great importance in clarifying my role as a Christian. Don Postema, the chaplain, was also supportive, and Greta and I have deeply valued his friendship, along with that of his wife Elaine. The support of the larger church through the challenges of the Christian Art Show was invigorating to me. Having a small group of individuals who were willing to listen and nurture me was an invaluable aid in my survival as an art student, and in many ways this is still true for me as an artist. I need a small support group around me who will affirm me as a Christian and as an artist. It is not the number of people but the quality of the relationship that counts.

At the University of Michigan there were almost no graduate students to whom I could relate, for I was not living the kind of life they were living; their values were not my values, and they were not doing what I was doing in the studio. The only exception to that was Harry Hansen. Harry had worked in landscape painting and was exploring new ways of working, just like me. We often talked about our goals and experiences and discussed our works with each other. Our friendship continued for many years, even though we were many miles apart when Harry took a position at the University of South Carolina. For the most part, though, interaction in the program was minimal. Critiques were held on an individual basis, between the graduate student and the graduate professor. As a result there was no communal opportunity to talk or to share, except what we did informally as fellow students. In addition, not all graduate students were working in the communal space. Some had their own studio spaces elsewhere, which made it even harder to know what they were doing. At the end of the semester, when all of us graduate students had to display our work for a faculty review, there was a brief opportunity to see what the others had done. But, as already mentioned, my graduate professors — Bill Lewis, Al Mullen, Frank Cassara, and Emile Weddige — played an important part in my shaping as an artist during my time at the University of Michigan.

An Affirmation

I completed my degree requirements in May of 1966 and received my Master of Fine Arts (MFA) degree from the University of Michigan with a major in printmaking and a minor in painting. I was now recognized as a fine artist and had a degree to prove it. It was all too unreal, too unbelievable, and yet it was true. Even today when I look back, I am amazed about the whole thing. From grease monkey to fine artist — what a surprising turn of events! But the Lord was not done yet; he had some more surprises in store for me.

President Spoelhof had officially established the Calvin College Art Department in 1965. Before then Edgar Boevé and Robin Jensen had been members of the Education Department. In the fall of 1965, Boevé gave a presentation about art in the Ann Arbor University Chapel, and afterwards he talked with me about Calvin College. He invited me for an interview. I met with the other members of the department, the dean, the president, and the professional status committee. In February of 1966, the Board of Trustees interviewed me. Forty or so ministers, representing the various classes of our denomination, questioned me about art. It was an unforgettable experience, and I still remember portions of that interview today. President Spoelhof told me afterwards that the interview had gone well. The Board of Trustees appointed me that afternoon to be an instructor in art at Calvin College.

The year of our Lord, 1966, was a special year in my life. In that year I became a U.S. citizen; I completed the work for the MFA degree; I received an appointment to teach at Calvin College; Greta was expecting our first child; we bought our first house; and we welcomed my Dutch parents (whom Greta had never met) for the first time into our home. We were truly blessed. Maybe it is not strange in the United States to go from grease monkey to art professor, for, after all, the American dream is to go from paperboy to president. But there had been no indication that my life would turn out this way. As with many things, it is only in retrospect that we can recognize — with amazement and gratitude — how the Lord has worked in our lives.

In the front of my Dutch Bible is a note from my mother, which says:

Aan onze Jan. Ter Gedachtenis aan Uw Belijdenis op
Zondag 16 Jan, 1955. Ps 119:105.
Je dankbare Ouders,
>   *Jan Overvoorde, A. D. Overvoorde den Braber*

Translated:

To our Jan in remembrance of your confession on
Sunday, January 16, 1955. Psalm 119:105.
Your grateful parents,
>   *Jan Overvoorde, A. D. Overvoorde den Braber*

I still have that Bible and use it from time to time. The text from Psalm 119 — "Thy word is a lamp to my feet and a light to my path" — became our wedding text in 1962. In 1955 it was customary in our Dutch church for the minister to select an appropriate text for each of the young people who made public profession of faith. So I too received a text, albeit a strange one. I was given just three words from John 1:46: "Come and see," which was the reply Philip gave to Nathanael when he asked him about Jesus of Nazareth. I remember some of the discussions about the assigned text after the service at our home during coffee time. This strange text didn't seem related to my current life as a soldier, nor did it seem connected with my earlier life as a diesel mechanic. No one could figure it out. "Come and see" did not seem to fit me.

But as I said before, the way the Lord works is often a mystery. He knows so much and we know so little. The Lord leads and calls, guides and directs when we least expect it. He is forever near and stands ready in times of trouble and in times of joy. I can see this now, looking back, for in retrospect the words from John 1, "Come and see," given to me when I professed Christ as my Savior, have become a perfect fit, a motto for my life. All I needed to do was "come and see," and recognize the Lord's doing. I had to learn to trust him and simply follow him, even if it took me across an ocean and half a continent.

Chapter Three

The Calling and Task of the Artist

Each one should use whatever gift he has received to serve others.

1 Peter 4:10

Discovering the Call

It seems appropriate that when we talk about artists, we talk about a calling. It is not just ministers who talk about their special calling of spreading the good news of the gospel. Other individuals, like artists, talk about their calling as well. To accept a call of any kind, no matter what the task, will require courage and commitment. Becoming an artist is not an easy undertaking; besides courage and commitment, it demands a great deal of discipline. A calling may vary from a direct challenge and acceptance to a slow realization that one is meant to serve the Lord in a particular way. Some people, for example, grow up in a rich cultural environment where they are surrounded by art objects and challenged to participate in artist-nurturing discussions. Such individuals may develop a deep appreciation of the arts or even become artists themselves. For others there is no such nurturing cultural environment; none of the family members may show any natural talents or interest in the arts. In my own case, as I have related in previous chapters, there was a slow process of becoming, rather than an early conviction that I should be, an artist.

When I was a youngster I knew nothing about art, nor did I know any artists. To have a conviction, one first needs to know something about the subject. When I attended Kendall School of Design to become a visual designer, I became more aware of the role of the fine artist. However, I did not yet know what that meant, or what it implied or required. Returning to school was an opportunity to improve the quality of my life, to train for a more suitable and better-paying job. At the time, my understanding of the fine arts was very limited, and I was certainly unaware of what it meant to be a Christian artist. As I learned more about art and discovered the role that artists have played in the past, it began to dawn on me that maybe I was called to serve as an artist. I was a confessing Christian, having made public profession of my faith in Christ in 1955. After you make that public profession, you soon begin to realize that as a young Christian you are in the process of becoming, for there is still so much to learn. While attending the University of Michigan, I began to realize that I was also in the process of becoming an artist. That realization led to the questions, Is this my calling? Have I been given a special task?

In my room at home in the Netherlands with some of the drawings done in the early 1950s

The idea of a special task for the artist is not unique. In Exodus 31:1-5 we read:

The Lord said to Moses, "See, I have called by name Bezalel, the son of Uri, son of Hur, of the tribe of Judah. And I have filled him with the Spirit of God, with ability and intelligence, with knowledge and all craftsmanship, to devise artistic designs, to work in gold, silver, and bronze, in cutting stones for setting, and in carving wood, for work in every craft."

Here is an artist filled with the Spirit. He is not a priest, not a prophet, not a king, but an artist. Bezalel is one of the first individuals mentioned in the Old Testament as having received the Spirit of God. Filled with the Spirit to do what? To make art! Bezalel was to build the tabernacle and all the objects in and around it. In the King James Version it says that the Spirit endowed him with workmanship, knowledge, and wisdom. The artist who built the tabernacle needed all three, for it was not enough for him to have craftsmanship (one who uses his hands). It was not enough for him to have craftsmanship and knowledge (one who uses his hands and his head). No, for Bezalel to be an artist, he needed craftsmanship, knowledge, and wisdom. Wisdom is knowledge of God. So the true artist employs his hands, his head, and his heart. This story is a wonderful affirmation of the task of the artist and his or her special place within the community.

Not all of us, however, are as clearly appointed and inspired as Bezalel. Bezalel was clearly called by God himself. After I left the University of Michigan to accept my task at Calvin College, I was quite convinced that I was called to be an artist. That belief was called into question, however, one Sunday morning when Rev. Andy Kuyvenhoven preached a sermon at Grace Church as a guest preacher. In that sermon Rev. Kuyvenhoven said: "No, you are not called to this or that profession, you are called to be a Christian. You are called to the office of believer." At first it was hard for me to accept that sermon. I struggled with it, because it did not provide me with answers to the question of what one should do with one's life. How do you go on? How do you select a career as a Christian? Moreover, many of the students I was advising came to me struggling with that very question. I needed to find a way to complete the sermon, a way to connect the calling of a Christian with the life a person is to live.

Adopted in Christ

Before this sermon, I had believed that I was special because I was called to be an artist. Now I learned that I was special, not because I was an artist, but rather because I was adopted. God the Father adopted me; he made me Christ's brother. The idea of being adopted is very real to me for several reasons. The first is that Greta and I adopted two biracial children. Joy Anne came to us as a baby in 1970, and Peter Sebastiaan arrived in our house in 1974 when he was three months old. Joy and Pete have been part of our family from the very moment they arrived. They are our children, just as Sonja, born in 1966, and Paul, born in 1968, are our children. So we have learned what adoption means in a special, personal way. We also learned about adoption when we joined Grace Christian Reformed Church in Grand Rapids. When we returned to Grand Rapids in 1966 and were looking for a new home church, we discovered that, unlike most Christian Reformed Churches in Grand Rapids at that time, Grace Church

The Overvoorde family in 1982. First row: Chris Stoffel, Nel, Mom, Dad, Geri, Dick. Back row: Toon, Adri, Chris, Nico, Joop.

needed members. We were the nineteenth family to join Grace Church and were only the second white family to become members. We discovered what it meant to be adopted into a family of believers who eventually meant more to us than our own brothers and sisters. My brothers and sisters, after all, were 3,500 miles east, and Greta's brothers and sisters were 2,500 miles west of us. We did, of course, correspond with our blood brothers and sisters; I wrote home weekly for twenty years, and Greta wrote to her family regularly. But through adopting our children and becoming part of our church family we discovered that adoption means a living relationship that requires priorities. When you care about someone, that person becomes important to you, often more important than yourself. When you are adopted by the Father, it means that Christ comes first, first in everything. Your fellow brothers and sisters in Christ will also receive a high priority in your life. But the biggest lesson of all for me was that if Christ comes first in everything, then art will always be second, not first.

Rev. Kuyvenhoven's sermon also led me to realize that when you are a Christian, you need to live in a way that lets you grow and mature as a Christian. God has made each of us unique, and that means that each of us has to figure out for ourselves how we are different. The idea that no two of us are alike can be illustrated with this classroom experience. Teaching students how to draw faces was always a unique challenge. First we discussed an ideal face with all the proper proportions and relationships. When all the students had drawn an ideal face, they would then be challenged to draw another student's face. They would observe and even measure the other person's face in order to discover how the other person's face deviated from the ideal face. What applies to our own facial features also applies to our whole person. Discovering how we deviate can be a healthy exercise for all of us.

Discovering the Gifts

God has endowed each of us with special gifts, with interests and inclinations. Sometimes circumstances and lack of opportunity may not allow us to nurture and develop all of our special gifts the way we would like. At other times we'll find that God leads and uses us in amazing ways, allowing us to discover gifts we didn't know we had. God is, after all, a Lord of surprises. Later, I will discuss in more detail how we function as artists within a community, but for now let it be clear that we all have special gifts, artist and non-artist alike. Special gifts need to be tested, explored, and developed. If we use our special gifts to serve others, the way God intended it to be, we will give glory to his name. The apostle Peter talks about the use of gifts in 1 Peter 4:10-11:

> Each one should use whatever gift he has received to serve others, faithfully administering God's grace in its various forms. If anyone speaks, he should do it

Printing the woodcut
Communion, *late 1966*

as one speaking the very words of God. If anyone serves, he should do it with the strength God provides, so that in all things God may be praised through Jesus Christ. To him be the glory and power for ever and ever. Amen.

Discovering our special gifts entails a challenge: to serve others, we need to hone and test and master the discipline required to use our gifts well. When we do, we learn much by experience; we find that we like to do some things more than others because we do them well. Exploring our natural interest is a way to begin the process. Education will provide opportunities and experiences that will help us realize who we are and what our gifts are.

Learning about my special gifts was a slow process, a process that took years to develop and mature. Eventually it meant that, for me, the best way I could be a thankful, living-in-Christ kind of being was to be an artist. That became the application of the sermon on Christian calling: I was called to be a Christian, and the best way I knew how to be a Christian was to be an artist. Since I have realized this, I have used this idea many times in class and in advising sessions. The special gifts God has given each of us sets us apart from each other. Each of us has to respond individually to God's calling to become a Christian. A true life of thankfulness is a life lived to its fullest potential, employing all the gifts with which God has endowed us, serving God and his people just as Bezalel did in the building of the tabernacle.

The Nature of Our Gifts

When you are a Christian, you will respond to God's world and to his Word. As Christian artists, we need to recognize that God's Word and world precede us, and all we can do is affirm, clarify, select, rearrange, elaborate, or testify to what was before. We respond to what already was and is. As Bruce Lockerbie writes in his book *The Liberating Word*:

> God gave Man none of his own omnipotence to create ex nihilo, but he did expect Man to arrange and rearrange the components of beauty in an ever more pleasing form. (34)

An artist does not create anything from nothing. God is the initiator and originator of everything. He is the true creator and we are only re-creators. As the Preacher says in Ecclesiastes:

> *What has been will be again,*
> > *what has been done will be done again;*
> > *there is nothing new under the sun.*
> *Is there anything of which one can say,*
> > *"Look! This is something new"?*
> *It was here already, long ago;*
> > *it was here before our time. (1:9-10)*

For many years modern art has been defined mostly in terms of originality and inventiveness. The concept that we are just re-creators relieves us from this modern-art burden of striving to be original, inventive, or unique. God has made each of us unique already. All we have to do is be ourselves, to respond in our own unique, personal manner. I used to tell my students a Dutch saying that goes something like this: "Doe maar gewoon, dan doe je gek genoeg," which translates into: "Just be yourself, that's unusual enough." Art students and many artists think they have to work at being special because they do not recognize that they are already. God has made them so. Moreover, the way we see as Christian artists has been altered by the recognition of who God is, what he has done, and what he is doing in this world. Bruce Lockerbie describes it this way:

> The Christian writer is an artist who brings the life of Christ to his art, enhancing it with the brilliance of faith, the warmth of love, the certitude of hope. Such a vision affects his art, giving him a new perspective on the human situation because he now sees it with the help of divine illumination. (23)

As visual artists we need to recognize one more important element, and that is that when we attempt to visualize, we need materials. Materials are at the heart of what the artist does: manipulate stuff. The way we use materials may depend upon what we choose to portray initially, what tools and other materials we add in the process, and what medium we choose to work in. But as visual artists we need to recognize that God is the giver, the source of all things; not only the Word and the world but also the materials we use are God-given. The brushes, paints, canvas, paper, pencils — all are provided by God. All we can do is to respond by using these gifts in an appropriate manner.

Art as a Response

The nature of that response is special and rich, in my view, for it is my prayer, my act of worship. I do not always need words to pray, nor is it always

*The Extent Some People
Will Go To . . . , 1968,
color woodcut, 36″ diameter
(Collection of Peace Lutheran
Church, Sparta, Michigan)*

essential that I use words to worship. When I work the image, I reveal my thoughts, my adoration, my feelings, because God made me. As artists we need to learn and accept that what we do is a visual response rather than a verbal one. To me it is not unlike the experience I have when I partake of the Lord's Supper. My partaking does not so much depend on words as on the sense of smell and taste to remember that the Lord has died for me.

When we worship God, we enter into a dialogue. Sometimes God speaks back to us through a sermon, sometimes through a song, sometimes through an observation, and occasionally through the recognition of an idea or an image. Over the years I have learned that God will surprise me when I work. He will allow me to discover new things, new insights, and greater clarity.

Preparation in the Basics

Bezalel's task was to master with his hands, to understand with his head, and to experience with his heart. When I was 12 years old, I was taught to use my hands in certain ways as I learned the craft of a metal worker. We learned to cut, file, stamp, grind, drill, shave, mold, and remold metal, using tools held mostly with our own hands. Looking back I am grateful, for I was respected for my trade. My trade gave me a personal identity. I was somebody when, at the age of 14, I completed my trade school training and was hired as a metal worker. I was taught at a young age that to use my hands was a noble thing.

The kind of training I received in the Netherlands is not available in the United States. The number of skill centers is limited, and trade schools as I knew them do not exist here. The skill centers that do exist are often stigmatized and portrayed as problematic. The joy and satisfaction of mastering a trade is therefore denied to many who could benefit from acquiring a meaningful trade. High schools have become places where students prepare for college or take general courses with no particular aim at all; few are challenged to learn a trade. This lack of trade schools is also problematic for art students, because they do not have an opportunity to acquire the basic skills at an early age. Artists of the past were often apprenticed with a master

At the opening reception of my first solo exhibition in the St. Cecilia Building, Grand Rapids, Michigan, in 1962

as early as age 9 or 10. Talented students could start their career as artists at an early age. Anthony Van Dyck (1599-1641), for example, was a full master at the age of 16 and became one of the leading artists of the Baroque period. Many others in the history of art and music created masterpieces before they reached the age of 25.

As for the training of young artists today, we need to recognize that the basic skills are essential if a person is to succeed in art. Every skill mastered will free the student from the tyranny of doing things only one way. Every additional medium mastered will allow the student another choice. Every different manner of working will free the student from narrow restrictions. The discipline of skill is essential for every visual artist, just as it is for the pianist or the vocalist in music. The curriculum for the artist needs to begin with the basics in drawing and design to teach the student how to see and how to organize what is seen. The various media will teach different things about process. For example, painting requires a direct manipulation of materials, whereas printmaking requires a more indirect way of creating an image. Sculpture manipulates various materials in subtractive, additive, and constructive ways to discover things three-dimensional. Working with ceramics creates three-dimensional images specifically in clay. Photography too is an indirect process that records and manipulates images using light rather than materials. Computer-generated images, on the other hand, are manipulated with no material involvement of any kind. Each medium is unique and requires different sensitivities and skills. It is important for young artists to discover what they are best at. That can happen only when they experience as many media as possible.

Art as a Way of Seeing

To gain knowledge and understanding may mean something different for the art student than for the philosophy student. There are different ways of knowing even within the academy, and not all the different ways of knowing are equally encouraged or recognized. Having ideas about images, for example, does not make you an artist. A philosopher uses images constantly to communicate a concept or an idea, but that kind of use of images does not make him an image-maker. Having the ability to discern differences between objects or patterns does not make you an artist either, for that is what many botanists do every day when they study various species and subspecies of plants. Recognizing that images have power does not do it either, for those who study popular culture know all too well from their motivational studies and surveys that such power exists. But this is not the same as knowing how to make images.

The artist's need to understand images is therefore different from all of the above examples. The illustrations used above show how images can be used; they say nothing about *creating* images. I submit that even many art historians are unfamiliar with how images are created. They speak eloquently about artists but seldom explain how a work of art really works, how it is constructed, how its inner relationships form a coherent whole, how it functions visually. That artists see different things when they approach a work of art was recently brought home to me at a national conference on Jan Vermeer. Henry Luttikhuizen, the art historian at Calvin College, and I were discussing one of the works in the Vermeer exhibit in Washington, D.C. I was pointing out to him how the blue was distributed throughout the work, how the blue graciously moved from one area to another area, creating a unity and a harmony that was quiet and reflective. It was the underlying structure that revealed the heart of the painting. One of the leading scholars on Vermeer was standing behind us, fascinated by what I was saying. His response was: "You must be an artist." We introduced ourselves, and he said to me: "Thank you for your insights."

Since my retirement I have become a volunteer at the Grand Rapids Art Museum, where I now present gallery walks. The responses of people during and after these gallery walks have also pointed out to me that what I see as an artist is not what they expected to see. These experiences have confirmed my belief that the way we see as artists needs to be shared. The way we see is based upon years of experience in creating images. Each of these experiences has taught us something about the world. As artists we need to claim boldly that our way of learning by doing gives us a different and valuable way of seeing. Others need to accept and respect that our way of seeing and knowing our world is an important element of our human understanding.

Another thing that distinguishes artists' experience of the world is that they are able to isolate incoming visual stimuli. They are able to select, and then play with the essential elements and principles that, in turn, allow them to make sense of this world. An artist does that by asking visual questions: What combination of colors, shapes, values, or lines will help clarify the issue? The artist needs to arrange, rearrange, view the results, and judge if this indeed defines what he or she is after. It is in the process of searching for an answer to a visual problem that the artist learns and discovers. The answer emerges from an inner dialogue between artist, idea, and materials.

Sometimes this dialogue within the artist is baffling to others. For example, I had a lot of trouble convincing the mathematicians who attended a mathematics colloquium at Calvin College of this kind of total visual approach. My presentation was about Maurice Escher, a Dutch graphic artist who made marvelous visual puzzles that contradicted or challenged our perception. The mathematicians were convinced that he was consciously illustrating one of their mathematical concepts instead of exploring the world visually and applying what I call the "what if" factor. But Escher was a visual explorer who used the visual response as his working method: What if I continue this line, or flip this shape?

The act of painting is often like that. For when I stand in front of that big, white canvas, each new stroke is dependent on the previous stroke. At the same time, I need to be aware of how that new stroke affects the whole surface of the painting. A stroke can be thick or thin, long or short, bold or delicate, light or dark. I have to decide what kind of stroke it will be. I have to do it, see the results, and think of the next move while still thinking about the whole. I am therefore involved in a constant process of decision making. It requires my whole being: my conscious and my unconscious being, my emotional as well as my rational being participate in that process. And I don't always know where it's taking me; I don't know the exact results in advance. The creative process entails much trial and error and comes with no guarantee of success. But it is a way for me to gain insight into and knowledge of this world. Doing seventy paintings of trees gave me a unique opportunity to explore and reflect on that part of God's creation. Painting these trees in an exploratory manner allowed me to connect with trees beyond their mere visual appearance. The etching "From Weeping to Fruitbearing" (see page 33) came at the end of that exploration, connecting my visual exploration with my theological inclinations. An artist may begin with a general notion, a broad concept. By playing with that concept in a visual manner, new insights may emerge, a new way of thinking about the concept and hence about the world.

The artist's way of thinking is, therefore, quite different from the analytical mind of the mathematician or the explanatory mind of the physicist or the botanist; it is also different from the logical mind of the philosopher or the theologian. The difference could be described as the difference between the Greek and Hebrew sense of knowing. The one assumes knowledge gained through the process of thought; the other assumes knowledge gained from experience. At one CIVA (Christians in the Visual Arts) conference, Betty Edwards, author of the book *Drawing on the Right Side of the Brain,* provided excellent insight into how artists think. Paul Vitz, a New York psychiatrist, spoke about the two sides of the brain and what happens when you separate them. When both speakers were finished, I asked the question: When does true creativity take place? Paul Vitz answered that it happens when both sides of the brain are in harmony, each balancing the other. For the beautiful truth is that all beings are endowed with an artistic and scientific way of thinking, with a right and left brain, with a Greek and Hebrew sense of knowing; and the two interact in mysterious ways. To be sure, scientific discoveries are not devoid of an artistic dimension; neither are artistic creations devoid of a rational dimension. But it is fair to say that the artist's way of thinking is not primarily analytical or explanatory or logical.

Much research has been done in recent years about how we process information and experiences. Cynthia Ulrich Tobias in her books *The Way We Work* and *The Way They Learn* talks about the different ways in which all of us gather and process information. Each of us is different and therefore we learn differently. And that is not always clear to us, because, as she states: "You will discover that identifying and understanding individual learning styles is an ongoing journey of observations and impressions" (*The Way We Work,* 6). She provides the following guidelines: observe, listen, experiment, focus, and learn. When I read these words, I was reminded of the words I used in my art classes when I tried to help my students find a subject to paint or draw. These guidelines can easily be adapted to doing art. Tobias further subdivides these categories: "Concrete Sequential, Abstract Sequential, Abstract Random, and Concrete Random are the strongest perceptual and ordering abilities. Each of us has a dominant style or styles that give us a unique blend of natural strengths and abilities" (*The Way They Learn,* 18). That is true for the artist as well.

D. Bruce Lockerbie talks about it this way:

> Imagination, memory, and dreams are more than passive storage areas within us. They are also the active forces working upon our consciousness through which we receive the stimulus for art. Of course, some scientists would disagree. The purely mechanistic behaviorist sees the brain as an organ responsive to electrical impulses, not unlike the computers in his lab. . . . The biochemist may have another explanation. He may look for stimuli from the body's nervous system, circulatory system, and digestive system. Depending entirely on how the artist "feels," his product will be bright and splashy or somber and brooding. (*The Liberating Word,* 15)

We do not, however, rely only on our "feelings." I reject the notion that "art is the expression of our emotions," a phrase that was popular in the 1950s and '60s, especially in art education. For the emotions are only one part of the complex process of learning and discovering. In his book *Lifelong Learning and the Visual Arts,* Donald Hoffman states:

> True immersion in the arts — whether directed towards the visual arts, drama, instrumental or vocal music, or creative writing and poetry — requires more than technique mastery or successful manipulation of materials. True creativity, an act of thinking process, requires an individual to have openness of thought (intellectualism) and a lack of fear from ridicule (self-concept); it imparts dignity to life. (7)

Hoffman's idea of an act of "thinking" that requires "openness" is a useful one. I believe that artists do a special kind of thinking when creating. Creativity involves one's total being. All that has been learned will come to bear upon that process, once it is engaged. We need to go beyond the appearance of things and seek out the underlying connections and discover the deeper meaning. John Dewey in his book *Art as Experience* describes it as an "impulsion." Dewey points out that it is not an instantaneous emission like turning on a light, but that it requires time and effort to produce a meaningful image. It takes time to digest, to acquire, to understand, to play with the possibilities. In our instantaneous age it is sometimes hard to accept such requirements. We would prefer for the intuitive process to produce instant results. When I suggested to my students that they make ten paintings to explore an idea, they protested loudly. They could not accept that any good idea was worth looking at for more than a moment of inspiration. Their intended approach was to put all they knew about a subject into one painting. When they were forced to abandon that approach for one semester, they began to discover that creating meaningful images requires much more exploration for gaining insight.

This is a special way of working, of learning by doing and seeing the emerging work connect with a variety of possibilities. Sometimes I have called myself a visual connection-maker. A work of art, be it a painting or a poem, a film or a photograph, must connect beyond the subject matter of the piece. These special new connections may lead us to a different way of looking at nature, to a modified perspective on the human predicament, or to a new way of interacting with another person. I don't know ahead of time what those new connections may be, for it is a process filled with mystery. The history of art is filled with works of art that have the ability to move us deeply. I don't know exactly how it works, nor do I know how to create these connections, these levels of meaning. All I do know is that it is hard work, requiring commitment, skill, and experience.

For me the process begins with the simple recording of what I see so that I can begin to understand the various components of a given landscape. Occasionally such drawings are the final product. Most often they are the first step. What follows must reach beyond the initial drawing, reach deeper, and hopefully make additional connections.

Other artists, however, just sit in the landscape soaking it up and then produce a painting from beginning to end in their studio. I know that Armand Merizon, a Grand Rapids landscape artist, often works this way. My college colleague Norm Matheis, with whom I would go out to paint directly in the landscape, approached it in a totally different way. Together Norm and I, after some driving around, would select a spot. I would set up, eager to record what looked like a possible image. Norm would sit and study the scene. After a while he would take his field easel, turn his back on the scene, and begin to paint. To me this was a perplexing approach. His explanation was that he needed to be inspired by the scene, and then, once he was inspired, he could paint anything. Each artist needs to discover what method of working will allow him or her to make works that are filled with mystery and meaning.

No amount of theology or philosophy of aesthetics can help you in the act of making an image. Some artists have the ability to envision a final image in their mind before they begin. They will search and work to achieve that very image. Others, on the other side of the spectrum, have only a vague idea or concept with which to begin. As a teacher it was my challenge to bring out the best in each of my students, regardless of their approach.

Virginia Bullock, director of exhibitions at the Center Art Gallery, wrote these words about me in a small booklet produced at my retirement and in connection with an exhibit of my former students called "Kunstfeest Diversity":

> In the body of work shown by Overvoorde's students and friends, there are no Overvoorde clones. Rather, there are personal and varied images which reveal the individual perspectives and convictions of the art makers. Overvoorde's students remember how he took the pressure off all beginners by emphasizing

Drawing in the Black Hills of South Dakota in the summer of 1989

the learning process, demonstrating how to use the media with patience and technical authority, while suggesting how to think about possible themes. He presented the life of an artist as one of continuing development and challenges; he was going through it himself. . . . The Professor allowed his pupils to be enterprising, rather than boxing them into regimented assignments. His students considered it a great compliment to be encouraged in the evolution of their own voice and identity. Never telling individuals exactly what to change in a project, he shared his variant perspectives for them to consider, allowing them to make their own choice.

To be comfortable with the activity is essential in my view. Which medium will allow for the greatest freedom of exploration? To discover the most suitable way of working, to master a fitting technique, to find the medium allowing for the strongest expression — this should be the goal of every art student. Each artist has to discover what subject is best expressed in what medium and what size is best for a given idea or project.

My Work as a Painter and a Printmaker

As a landscape painter I have learned that for me a painting starts with drawing. Drawing is a way of seeing for me, a way of understanding and a way of claiming a moment. It is my way of collecting information and doing research. I start by making a small sketch on the spot. Sometimes I add color notes along the side of the sketch. It is a quick record of what I saw at the time. When we travel, I do a watercolor that night based upon the simple drawing, thus strengthening my memory of the scene. Later, when I have returned to the studio, I may make a larger drawing that explores the composition and renders more of the details. On occasion I will use a photo to provide additional details. But I have found that the distortion of the lens, the overabundance of detail, and the inability of film to record the right color are a hindrance rather than a help in the creative process. What I saw and still see in my drawing is simply not what the photo shows. On the basis of the initial sketch and the subsequent drawings, I will make a painting, using either oil or watercolor as the medium.

With my prints I use a different method and approach. To start my woodcuts, I do some initial research so that I know with what and with whom I am dealing. If it is a biblical character, for example, I consult Jewish and Christian scholarly writers. Their perceptions and insights are essential for my initial understanding. Sometimes the research includes visual elements as well, like objects, costumes, and environments. After the research is completed, I do small compositional sketches, exploring the visual organization. When I am convinced of the basic divisions of black and white, I turn to the block and make my initial drawing directly on the block with brush and India ink. This is not the final image, because the brush marks need to be interpreted by the carving tools. Each carving tool leaves a distinctive mark when it is used. The final image is therefore defined by these marks. Each step is a translation into a more definable state, a progression toward a final image. Most of my religious images have been done in a print medium. The indirect process of the printing medium has best suited my exploration and finalization of such meaningful images.

I have tried to make paintings of the religious characters portrayed in my prints, but so far the results, compared with the prints, have been less than satisfying to me. When I have tried to make prints of the landscapes, I have also been dissatisfied most of the time. The print medium has been best suited for my religious images, and the watercolor, acrylic, and oil media have been well suited to my landscape paintings. Each medium has its own characteristics, makes its own demands, and defines its own limitations for each individual artist. Fittingness of medium is therefore another important factor for the young artist to discover. Each one needs to find a place within a medium, a comfortable place in which the process can be maximally productive and meaningful.

I have suggested before that what we see is altered by what we believe. Our Christian commitment modifies our vision. Our special interests are

Rain on the Peigan
Reserve, Alberta,
drawing, 20″ × 20″

served by how we work and play. The book of nature is very important to me as a landscape painter. How I should look at nature is a recurring question, for in the landscape I see the hand of God at work. Article 2 of the Belgic Confession reaffirms that belief:

By which means is God made known unto us?

   We know Him by two means: First, by the creation, preservation, and government of the universe, which is before our eyes as a most elegant book wherein all creatures, great and small, are as so many characters leading us to see clearly the invisible things of God, even His everlasting power and divinity, as the Apostle Paul says (Romans 1:20). All which things are sufficient to convince men and to leave them without excuse. Second, He makes Himself more clearly and fully known to us by His holy and divine Word, that is to say, as far as is necessary for us to know in this life, to His glory and our salvation.

God makes himself known to us not just through the visible but also through the invisible. And indeed some artists such as Paul Klee have claimed that art's purpose is to make visible the invisible — in other words, not just realism, but a special kind of realism, a special way of looking at things that would bring out something of God's power, God's divinity. The simple recording of a landscape is therefore not enough for the true artist or for the photographer.

Above I have related how we are called as Christians and how the artist becomes a Christian artist because he or she is adopted by Christ, adopted to grow in Christ as a person and as an artist. Artists, like everyone else, are gifted; we all need to discover these gifts in the service of others so that we might live lives of thankfulness. As artists we testify to the Christian vision. We thankfully acknowledge that God is the creator and we are but re-creators, for even the materials we use are God-given. When we acknowledge his creative power, we recognize that what we make is a human response, a worshipful response, a visual response that involves our

The wall of drawings done in the summer of 1993 in the Gushul Studio, as Artist in Residence for the University of Lethbridge, Alberta, Canada

whole person. We need to master our skills, hone our visual thinking, and be open to new discoveries. We each need to discover our own way of working, just as I needed to discover how differently I work as a painter and as a printmaker. Finally, the task of the Christian artist is to reveal. In the next chapter we will discover the different ways in which we, as Christians who are visually sensitive, can serve God's people.

Chapter Four

The Artist and the Designer

Years ago, poets and artists used to do what public-relations people do now: glorify kings, praise heroes and beauty, and espouse causes.

Gene Thornton, quoted in *Art and Soul: Notes on Creating,* by Audrey Flack

A Question of Choice

Young persons who are drawn to the visual arts will need to explore the different paths open to them, preferably even before beginning college. Most young Christians who are gifted in the visual arts will face a tough choice between becoming either designers or artists. The values in some Christian communities would encourage young people to become designers or commercial artists in order to become productive, responsible members of society. Becoming an artist may be highly problematic in such communities for various reasons. Earning a living and obtaining financial security are serious concerns and may rank higher than using one's visual gifts or artistic inspiration. For Calvinists like myself, a strong sense of responsibility and work ethic may also make it hard to choose a career in the fine arts.

Because the need to be accepted and function properly within a community is of concern to all of us, becoming an artist may not be an easy choice. The letters of Vincent van Gogh reveal that he struggled his entire

71

artistic life with the question of his usefulness as an artist. He did not consider himself to be a "productive member of society." And in many Christian communities today, the same attitude persists. Artists are seen as, if not irresponsible, at least nonproductive, noncontributing. Even within the academic community the artist is tolerated rather than accepted. At least that has been my experience on numerous occasions these past thirty years.

As I've already related, I became a visual designer first. Being a recent immigrant with no financial resources forced me into that initial decision, and my interest and involvement in the fine arts came later. I would advise young people, if at all possible, to be trained as artists first, and only later, if they wish, to switch to visual design. Being trained as an artist provides a broader education that will help one function better as a designer, if one makes that choice later. Being trained as I was in a design school was a rather narrow educational experience. It prepared me well for the job market but did not teach me the broader perspective on art and design. Without that broader view, the position of the designer becomes problematic. I developed a job mentality toward my work. Each design task I undertook was a job that had to be done within a certain time frame and within other restrictions. These restrictions created within me a job mentality that said: get it done as quickly as possible. It was this job mentality that I found difficult to shed when I became a fine artist. So if one has a choice and can follow the fine art program first, do that, if at all possible.

Most college programs allow students to keep their options open until the junior year. College programs are a bit more open about these things than design schools or art academies. The decision as to what school to attend is therefore also an important one. Programs will vary, and some will be more flexible than others.

The Similarity between Artist and Designer

It is important to recognize that both the designer and the artist are visual communicators. They may function at different levels and in different manners, but in the end it will be something visual that does the communicating. The cover of a magazine, for example, may be a combination of words and images, but how the entire cover is organized will be of major visual concern to the graphic designer and the editor. A painting may also communicate either a subject, the content of a subject, or the way we experience some aspect of the subject. In all cases it is communicating something visually. Whenever I think about communication, I am reminded of my interview with the Board of Trustees of Calvin College. There was extensive questioning about art as a means of communication until I answered one question this way. (At that time, the Board consisted of some forty ministers.) "Reverend," I said, "do you not go up into the pulpit on Sunday morning and under the guidance of the Holy Spirit preach the good news of the Lord? Are you successful in communicating?" After that answer, communication was dropped as a subject. All of us, in one way or another, visually or verbally, are attempting to communicate.

Excellent work should be the aim of both the designer and the artist. It should not be assumed that there is a difference in quality between the two; good quality work is required of both, no matter if it is a painting commission, a commercial request for a price catalog, the design for a newspaper advertisement, or a spontaneous watercolor.

Sometimes we use the designations "designer" and "artist" in order to imply that there is a commercial side to the work of the designer but none to that of the fine artist. We even use the term "commercial artist." It is true that the designer will often work under contract or have a salaried position. Such remuneration agreements are established ahead of time. The artist, on the other hand, must attempt to establish a market for what he or she has already done. Both the fine artist and the designer will need to spend time on promotion and name recognition. Both will need to be involved in the commercial activities of their profession. Neither one is free from the market mentality of our culture. The commercial aspect, although different for each, is not what separates the artist from the designer.

Het Woord, *1967, mural, Heritage Hall, Calvin College, acrylic on plaster, 60″ × 336″*

The Difference between Artist and Designer

The difference between the artist and designer can be found in the way the two function within our complex multicultural society. Recognizing that there is a difference does not imply in any way, however, that one is better than the other. It may be more appropriate and beneficial within this context to discuss one's "fittingness." Does it fit better with your personality and gifts to be a designer or to be an artist? It may be a question of temperament. The designer, unlike the artist, seldom works alone. Even when designers are independent and self-employed, they are part of a team, as I will discuss in more detail below. Designers respond to assignments or requests made by others, whereas artists usually respond to things within themselves. Only in the case of commissions does an artist vary this typical pattern. Since designers work by assignment, they are usually employed in the art department of an advertising agency or a printing plant, and thus they have the security of a salaried position. Job security is therefore an important consideration when you think about fittingness. You should also consider how important it is to you to be considered a productive member of society; society at large will not question your usefulness as much when you are a designer.

The Role of the Designer

As someone who was employed as a graphic or visual designer for many years, I will describe that type of designer's work in order to elaborate more fully on how the designer functions.

The graphic designer's activities often begin with a client who has a need. The designer will translate that need into a product — a brochure, a catalogue, or some other printed piece. The product will end up being printed by individuals sometimes known, sometimes unknown, to the graphic designer. There are many hands in the production pot before a simple flyer reaches the possible purchaser. Moreover, graphic designers will often do their work within an art department. Such a department may be connected to a production plant, an agency, or a publishing company. Designers will be working together with art directors and others who will make the final decision as to how their work is used. Their training, therefore, needs to include a broad perspective on people and society. Solid liberal arts training will be needed as well as a good basic training in design and drawing. A healthy sense of community will be important for the designer to function properly. The designer also needs to know how visual communication works at many levels. Both the effect and impact of an image and its poten-

Clouds Over Helena, Ohio,
1984, oil on canvas,
48″ × 60″

tial to modify people's behavior need to be studied by the student designer. A thorough knowledge of the field of mass communication, both in theory and practice, is therefore essential for the design student if he or she is to function properly within that field as an image-maker. A serious commitment to and interest in solving visual communication problems, as well as personal creative growth, are essential for today's visual designer.

Nowadays, most graphic design work is done on the computer, and a working knowledge of this tool is essential to become a successful designer. Computers should be an integral part of the design student's program of study. The basic design and drawing skills, however, should not be minimized or sacrificed at the altar of the latest chip or the newest software. Such visualizing skills will allow for a quick visual development of an idea. Many designers are still beginning with a drawing pad rather than a monitor to see the visual possibilities and establish a direction before starting on the computer. You should explore how well you relate to working without materials. The computer has only a mouse and no materials to manipulate. Would-be graphic designers who feel that a computer monitor is a prison should perhaps seek other ways to use their gifts.

The graphic designer is basically a visual spokesperson who helps people put their ideas into a visual form. This form may become a printed piece, or it may be shown in other ways such as film, TV, or on a network. The designer is commissioned to work with others in order to accomplish this task. If the designer works for a firm, this is normally a salaried position. If not employed by a firm, the designer is called a freelancer. But whether employed by self or others, he or she has to work as a member of a team. Participants will vary, but if we make a list of those involved we begin to recognize the extent of the team. (The numbers in brackets represent the total number of people.) Initially there is the client (1), or clients. When the graphic designer has completed the design, it will go out to a printing sales representative (2) for a printer's quote (3-4). When the job goes to the printer, it will be prepared by the prep department, which can involve more computer work (5), film work (6-7), proofing (8), plate work (9), press preparation (10), pressman (11), folding and cutting (12-13), and shipping (14). If we add the people involved in the additional distribution, we would have even more than the fourteen already mentioned. Often the designer will follow up by having contact with at least the key players of the production team, like the sales representative, and by approving proofs and finalizing the print proof of the project. It is not unusual for a graphic designer to visit the press room to review and approve a press proof. Needless to say, a sense of timing, meeting deadlines, and working under pressure are all part of the designer's job.

The Design World

When we look around we begin to recognize that the task of the designer is not only to "sell stuff." We soon become aware that our world is filled with objects and environments that are designed by someone. From the chair we sit in to the way a TV set looks, from the shape of spoons to the pattern of the shirt you are wearing, a designer was involved in a process of selection that enriches our lives in numerous ways. Visual communication is becoming more and more part of our culture. This increased involvement has provided young designers with new challenges and opportunities. When I was trained as a visual designer, I was prepared to function as a graphic artist who did key-line and paste up. I seldom became involved in visual communication problems or in solving issues. In the two years that I worked as a visual designer, for example, we as a production department did only one four-color promotion piece. The rest of the time we created black-and-white and occasionally two-color pieces. Since then the field has changed dramatically. As a designer you will have unique opportunities to participate in this promising world of mass communication. Video presentations, web design, and film production teams are employing young people who are willing and able to function as visual problem solvers.

The world of design is influenced by society and a variety of trends. Fashion design is a good example: color schemes and length of skirts are forever changing, so it seems. Some things are in and other things are out. Interior designs are also constantly changing — color schemes, for example, or certain textures. The design world is not a static world; it keeps changing according to fashion or fads. It is an exciting, powerful world with many special challenges. But traditional values have changed as a result of the mass media.

Because the mass media hardly existed in the world of our grandparents and great-grandparents, painting and sculpture carried more weight: the weight of tradition, dreams, and social commemoration. That means that as a Christian artist I have to recognize that painting and sculpture, or whatever medium I am working in today, no longer has the place it once had. All you have to do is open up the entertainment section in any newspaper, and you will find more stories about the latest music or movie than about an art gallery exhibition. The power of the mass media on our society today is much greater than the influence of painting, printmaking, or sculpture was one hundred years ago. On TV and on the Internet the multimedia approach has become a "melting approach," melting written words with spoken words, photographic images with video footage, while fact is often intertwined with commentary. The mass media have emerged as the leaders in communication. So I can agree with Robert Hughes when he says that "the power of television goes beyond anything the fine arts have ever wanted or achieved" (14).

The Nature of Art

Fine artists work mostly alone. They select a subject and find a medium that will allow them to create a work of art. They will not have a deadline, except what they choose to impose on themselves. This freedom can be intoxicating, for it seems there are no limits to what the artist can do. Freedom, however, is always freedom within a context. The artists will be limited by their skills, their own interests and inclinations, and their own perceptions of the world in which they find themselves.

There has been a great deal of discussion within the art world about what is the proper function and role of the artist. Especially in America, the discussion has often been heated and sometimes mean and narrow. But if artists want to make a living, they need to connect with others in the community and engage in that discussion, a discussion that will focus especially on the nature of art. A quick glance will not allow one to get at its deeper meaning. It will require study and contemplation, analysis and insight in order to get to the various layers of meaning of a work of art, which is a physical object with its own scale and density. Its images are not grasped or understood quickly; meanings do not hover on the surface of the work. Art requires the long look. It must be analyzed, contemplated, returned to, examined in the light of its context and history. A work of art is layered and webbed with references to the inner and outer worlds that are not merely iconic. It can acquire (although it does not automatically have) a spiritual dimension, which rises from its power to evoke contemplation. Fine art is much more than an array of social signals and symbols employed by the mass media. Its social reach is smaller, but it finds the ground for its survival in being what the mass media are not.

For example, consider the woodcut called "Glory, Amen . . . ," which I produced in 1968. This 36″ round image was crafted by cutting away all that was white in the image from a block of wood. In this case there were many colors, and for each color there was a wood block. The first level of appreciation is in recognizing the technical complexities needed to achieve this image on paper. The entire printing process was done by hand with a wooden spoon and was therefore far removed from the fast page reproductions of the modern printing press.

The fact that it was cut by hand into a wooden block makes each image an original. A print by definition is a multi-original. The image is composed within a circle, which is divided into four parts. In the center is the image of

Glory, Amen . . . , *1968,*
color woodcut, 36″ diameter

a human fetus surrounded by a circle of seven doves. Behind those doves is the image of a cross, and in the four sections we can see a man, an ox, a lion, and an eagle. On the outside of these four images and the cross is another circle consisting of twenty-four figures. Radiating from the fetus outward are the colors of the rainbow. That is the description of the image of the color woodcut, and if one knows nothing about Judeo-Christian beliefs, one can still enjoy the image for its relationship, proportion, and presentation.

We could also formally analyze the relationship of one element to another. Within art we have the elements and principles of design, and we can in turn apply these to the work in question. How was line employed, how was shape used, how was texture an important element, how essential was value, or how unifying was color? All these are questions that will allow us to look closer and longer at the work, questions we would not normally pose about an advertisement.

If we are familiar with the Bible, we know that there are some wonderful references in Ezekiel and in Revelation about the glory of Christ. The whole idea of Christ leaving his princely position to come down to live among us is something we cannot grasp. It is too great to comprehend, and yet you are invited to consider what Christ did for us in his miraculous birth, his life, his death on the cross, his resurrection — but above all his faithfulness as expressed in the rainbow. A quick glance may have provided you with the image of the cross, and you may not have gone beyond that. But now you are contemplating what Christ left behind and what he returned to after he did what was asked of him. Now you note the twenty-four elders surrounding the image.

We could go on, for I am sure that if some of my theological colleagues were standing next to me, they would elaborate even more on the many theological implications. But I am not finished. There are still more layers, for we have not considered the source of the image. In the Gothic period, rose windows were often incorporated into the structure of a cathedral. In these marvelous stained-glass windows, it was the story of salvation that was often portrayed. These windows have always fascinated me, and I am sure that unconsciously I was inspired by these windows. Later I did another woodcut called "That Glorious Form . . . ," which is a simplified and also intensified look at the issue of Christ's birth. The whole question of Christ's birth is raised in these images because of the birth of our own children. Sonja was born in 1966 and Paul in 1968. Artists share and testify; they confess and they witness, sometimes intentionally and sometimes accidentally. The role of the artist has changed over the years. History has demanded different kinds of things from the artist in different ages. Each work of art is a particular response to the age in which it is produced, and at times, a particular response to events in the life of the artist.

The Art World

The Iconoclasts of the sixteenth century changed and challenged the traditional role of the artist. The history of the Reformation and its response to the arts is well documented. The Protestant part of the church no longer functioned as a supporter of the arts. As a matter of fact, it spoke forcefully against particular uses of the arts. In many ways it was made clear that artists were no longer welcome. Many of the visual codes, however, continued to function in general ways, not unlike the mass media do today. What fascinates me is that in the seventeenth century, in the Protestant United Provinces of what is now called the Netherlands, we find the Golden Age of Dutch painting. Artists like Rembrandt van Rijn, Frans Hals, Jan van Goyen, Jan Steen, Jan Vermeer, and many others were still painting religious subject matter besides wonderful portraits, landscapes, and genre paintings. Fortunately for the Dutch, many of these works remained in their country, thanks to private collectors.

But a quick review will show us how the role of art within the art world has changed and modified in recent decades. By the 1950s the dominant force in American art was the New York School and abstract expressionism. When I was at the University of Michigan, we discussed the

He Broke It . . . , *1984,*
drypoint, 15″ × 22″

Trees in Wind and Rain,
1965, watercolor, 22″ × 30″,
done while studying with
William Lewis

Top Wave, *1965, acrylic on paper, 30″ × 22″, done while studying with Allen Mullen (Collection of Rev. Richard Duifhuis)*

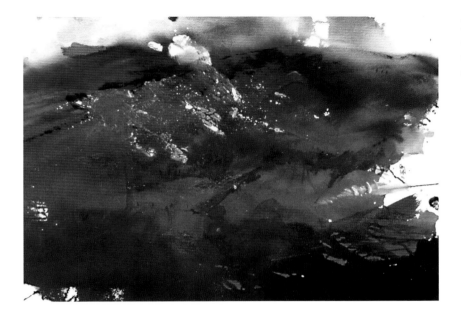

Blue Wave with Red, *1965,
acrylic on paper, 22″ × 32″,
done while studying with
Allen Mullen*

White Wave, *1965, acrylic
on paper, 22″ × 30″, done
while studying with Allen
Mullen*

The Struggle, *1962, oil on panel, 24″ × 24″. Now in the collection of Daniel De Graaf Galleries. This work received first place in the Christian Art Show of 1962.*

The Extent Some People
Will Go To . . . , *1968,*
color woodcut, 36″ diameter
(Collection of Peace Lutheran
Church, Sparta, Michigan)

Glory, Amen . . . , *1968,*
color woodcut, 36″ diameter

That Glorious Form . . .
forsook the courts of
everlasting day and chose
with us a house of mortal
clay . . . , *1968, color
woodcut, 36″ diameter*

Twelve Stones, *1975, acrylic*
on canvas, 36″ × 48″
(Collection of Mr. and Mrs.
Conrad Bradshaw)

Formation, 1977, acrylic on canvas, 36″ × 48″

Plowed Fields Near
Rotterdam, The
Netherlands, *1978,*
watercolor, 20″ × 30″

Near Lekkerkerk,
The Netherlands, *1978,*
watercolor, 22″ × 30″

Eerde Woods, The Netherlands, *1978, watercolor, 22″ × 30″ (Collection of Dr. Schulte Nordholt, The Netherlands)*

Clouds Near Adrian, Michigan, *1985, oil on canvas, 36″ × 60″*

Clouds Over Helena, Ohio,
1984, oil on canvas,
48″ × 60″

Skyscape near Shelby, Michigan, *1985, oil on canvas, 72″ × 60″*

Mid West Summer, *1985,*
oil on canvas, 66″ × 120″

Afterwards, *1986, oil on canvas, 66″ × 84″*

Sunday Morning, *1986,*
oil on canvas, 66″ × 96″
(Collection of the Prince
Corporation)

Lake Effect, *1986, oil on canvas, 66″ × 84″ (Collection of Reformed Bible College, Grand Rapids, Michigan)*

View from 520 towards
Claresholm, Alberta, *1993,*
watercolor, 22″ × 22″

Rain in the East, Near
Hillspring, Alberta, *1994,
diptych, oil on canvas,
48″ × 96″*

Moon and Clouds Near
Cowley, Alberta, *1994,*
oil on canvas, 48″ × 48″

Twelve Stones, *1990,*
oil on canvas, 60″ × 60″

Installation, "Ordinary Times," Grace Christian Reformed Church, Grand Rapids, Michigan, 1980s

*Installation, Grace
Christian Reformed Church,
for Easter Sunday Service,
1980s (right)*

THIS DO IN REMEMBRANCE OF ME

From Generation to
Generation: 150 Years of
Graafschap Christian
Reformed Church, *1997,
oil on canvas, 48″ × 60″*

works of such masters as Willem de Kooning, Jackson Pollock, Mark Rothko, Frans Kline, and Robert Motherwell. We appreciated their action brush works and barely recognized that, in the process, image, story, and three-dimensionalism were negated if not thrown out altogether. It was the drip, the dash, the splash, the dynamic stroke, the sagging of paint, and the shallow space that intrigued us. Few of us were interested in the realists of earlier decades, although as a Christian artist I was looking seriously at the work of Charles Birchfield. I was aware of Edward Hopper, Reginald March, Jack Levine, and even Andrew Wyeth.

In the sixties and seventies, the New York School reacted against abstract expressionism, and things changed so quickly that Jackson Pollock and Willem de Kooning became academic in one generation. There was pop art, op art, kinetic art, conceptual art, and minimalism. It was all very heady stuff for us in graduate school, and it was hard to keep up with the latest trends. Reductionism banished the picture frame, and works were often painted directly on the wall. Photographs were projected and copied. Realism itself became the real. Found objects were transformed into three-dimensional collages or glued into boxes. Installations became freestanding objects. Sculptures were cast from real people and made to look exactly like them when finished. I remember talking to what looked to me like a graduate student in art, at the Nelson Gallery in Kansas City. When I got no response, I recognized that I was talking to a sculpture piece. The idea became art, social and political commentary became an aesthetic of its own. Artists had ideas, which were constructed by metal workers. Instructions for work were typed out and sent to a museum for execution. Finally, words entered the world of the visual, replacing material manipulation. Where could you find your bearings in all this?

In the eighties, some representational painters like Mark Tamsey, Philip Pearlstein, Eric Fischl, Vincent Desiderio, Alex Katz, and George Tooker were fortunately flourishing side by side with the abstract expressionists

Bruce Marsden, Frank Stella, Agnez Martin, and Sol Lewitte. The confrontational mode of the earlier decades had mellowed. It was a bigger world now, and it appeared to be more open to various approaches and possibilities, including a greater acceptance of the spiritual. The question, however, remains: Where in the art world will you find your place?

I have said little about various techniques, for initially you will need to discover where your inclinations will lead you in terms of the various painting, printmaking, sculpture, or ceramic subdivisions. That is the challenge in your education — to discover your specific gifts within the complexity of art. You must discover your voice within yourself and within your community.

After you have begun to realize what kind of art you want to make and you have acquired the mastery of several techniques, you will still need to establish yourself within the art community in order to be effective in the general community. There are basically three different components to the art community: competitions and invitational exhibitions, commercial art galleries and the art market, and the art museums. Each has its own history, its own dynamics, and its own politics. It is therefore important to learn as much as possible about each of them in your area.

Local, state, and national competitions are good places to get a sense of how your work measures up to that of others. Please do not confuse your worth with that of your work. Entering competitions is a good way to build up a reputation. Many museums have annual juried exhibitions and the local media often recognize such exhibitions. In some instances the prize winner of a museum competition will receive a solo exhibition at a later time. Most art magazines will publish a list of upcoming competitions and give details about the event as to who can enter, and size, weight, and other restrictions on the entries. Many competitions today require slides as an initial selection device. It is therefore important to either learn how to make excellent slides or have someone else do it for you. Your first task, then, is to judge and select from among your own production. After you have completed your own selection process, test it out on others. Would they select the same works? Ask your teachers, your fellow students, your family members.

To be sure, juried shows have their negative sides. Judges are not always fair and impartial in the selection process; they may let their own preferences and views get in the way. I place the emphasis on selection rather than rejection. Receiving a card that says your work has been rejected instead of not selected is a more devastating experience in my view. I have received my share of rejection cards. It is not fun, but it is part of the process. I have also received my share of awards, and I have successfully participated in many competitions. Invitational exhibitions are initiated by educational galleries and art museums on a regular basis. They will often be conceived around a topic or a theme, and artists are selected on how their work will fit the theme. It is a different way of creating an exhibition.

After you have developed some name recognition because of juried exhibitions and you have participated in invitational and group exhibitions, commercial galleries may contact you to show your work. Gallery directors depend upon the success of artists to produce salable works, and artists depend upon the success of the gallery director to make the sale. Galleries are commercial ventures; they need to pay the rent, pay the insurance, pay for promotion, etc., while the only income is from the sale of works made by artists. They earn their percentages and deserve what they get. Most artists depend either on a gallery or several galleries to sell their work, or on museums to build a reputation. Some will sell their work as individuals, using a gallery/studio type of set-up. In all cases there is a dependency on the art market, a market over which the fine artist has little control. In this setting, you will need to spend time promoting your work. It is often true that you will do the promoting after you have created the work. You therefore need to establish a working relationship with either a gallery director or a representative, unless you have other income and do not need to live on what you make.

Moreover, the market is often fickle when it comes to supporting artists. To let the market dictate your production is therefore a dangerous route to take. As an artist, you need to keep asking what motivates you.

The role of museums has also changed a great deal over the last hundred years. Initially it was the private collector who collected works of art for his own pleasure. (The idea of investing in art for financial gain is a more recent development.) These collections were displayed in public places by local art organizations; eventually they would grow into a gallery, and after that it would be called a museum. That is very much what happened in Grand Rapids with the Grand Rapids Art Museum and in Muskegon with the Muskegon Museum of Art; the same is true for many other art institutions.

Thus, historically the care of private collections became a public affair and the need for a museum was established. Collecting works of art, however, is not without problems. On the one hand, collecting and preserving works from the past is a worthy goal, but how we display these works may distort their original intent. Works that originally were meant to assist worshipers within the walls of a cathedral are now on display in a museum hall. In this neutral museum hall, there is often no context and no connection with the original intent of the individual items. Moreover, many museums now organize major exhibitions in an attempt to attract visitors, as Robert Hughes observes:

> It has become a low rating mass medium of its own right. In doing so it has adopted, partly by osmosis and partly by design, the strategy of other mass media: emphasis on spectacle, cult of celebrity, the whole masterpiece-and-treasure syndrome. (398)

As a result, the museum's role and function have changed. It is not easy, for example, to contemplate a work when you are surrounded by three hundred other individuals within a small space. It is not unlike being in a full elevator and trying to get to the button for the right floor. Competition among the major institutions and cities is severe. Grand Rapids recently experienced this sense of competition when the Grand Rapids Art Museum mounted a major exhibition of the work of the Italian painter Perugino. Various reviews of this exhibition in the national press questioned how this fine show ended up in Grand Rapids. The latest conflict between Grand Rapids and the Eastern establishment was about the twenty-four-foot-high bronze horse created by Nina Akamu from drawings by Leonardo da Vinci for the Frederik Meijer Gardens. But such competition can yield important benefits. Civic pride in Grand Rapids as a result of these efforts has increased. Both the Grand Rapids Art Museum and the Meijer Gardens have played a major role in a renewed interest in art and other cultural activities.

You will want to learn about the local history of the museum in your area and what its involvement is not only with the "old masters" but also with what the nineteenth-century historians called the "living masters."

Conclusion

There are many ways in which the Christian artist-designer can function in our society. As a designer, one can function as maker of many things, from pamphlets to tools, from brochures to packages. The industrial designer becomes involved with the production of prototypes, which may range from toasters to automobiles. Today the film and video industry employs many people; some were originally trained as fine artists and some as designers. The computer industry also employs individuals to design web pages and other visual materials. Museums and other institutions employ people to design and make their displays. Art museums employ installation designers, and the medical profession sometimes employs illustrators to record medical procedures. Anthropologists and archeologists have used artists to record their findings. The list of how the artist-designer may be employed is long and varied, and the lines between the artist and the designer are not always clear. But your cultural mandate is clear: you must participate in the art world and test your work against the work of other artists. That is why I have encouraged you to enter works in juried exhibitions. We need to find our voice in this cultural world and contribute to the best of our ability.

Finally, you are called to be a Christian, and the best way you know how to be a Christian is to be an artist or a designer, a maker of visual things. For both the artist and the designer, it is a personal matter of faith that should be at the core of their being. You have the unique opportunity to serve all of us in a special way, but you have to remember that it is the Lord who gave you the gifts. All things, every square inch, says Abraham Kuyper, are under God's domain, and that means for me that God will use in his time and his way what I have done in his name. God will work among us, but not according to our dictates or our desires. Just because we have completed a major work and now feel the need to be affirmed, does not mean that God will do so. No, God does not work according to our whims. I am glad he does not. God will take our response, our visual testimony, our confessional visual declarations and our image-laden witnessing and make them perfect. Soli Deo Gloria!

Chapter Five

My Journey as an Artist

"Your word is a lamp to my feet and a light to my path."

Psalm 119:105

In Chapter 2, "My Initial Journey," I described my initiation and education in the arts. In this chapter I want to share what I have learned since then — doing art. Some of what I have learned I have already shared in the previous chapters, but much remains, for the doing of art has taught me many things.

You, along with every young artist, face many questions: How do you market your work? How do you build up a reputation so that your work can be shared with others? What should you look for in a relationship between a gallery director and an artist? How do you establish a direction? What should happen when you receive a commission? These are some of the issues I have faced, and I would like to share my experiences with you.

Building a Reputation

Even before I returned to school, Greta and I would often escape for a weekend to display some of my work in the various art fairs that were popular around the state of Michigan. There were some very good ones in the early and mid-sixties, and it was a way for us to test the market as well as to gain some tuition and art supply money. Some shows required slides to be submitted ahead of time. These slides would be reviewed by a committee to ensure the quality of the work to be displayed. There would often be a fee of some kind to participate in these shows. Every year the state of Michigan published a calendar that listed these outdoor art fairs. I believe other states do the same. That was the first public way we promoted and sold the works I produced. Before that I had sold some work to family and friends. It was a good way to gain exposure, to collect responses, and learn what it was like to sell my work.

Another way to test my work was to enter it in city and regional juried exhibitions. It took a certain amount of effort and money to participate, but it was well worth it. The entry fee and the framing could be costly, however. I remember what it cost me, back in the late sixties, in one show when I thought I had been successful. I want to use that experience as an illustration here, to show that even well-intentioned art organizations can make it hard for an individual artist to survive. The entry fee for the show was $10. I entered three prints, each valued at $40, and spent about $35 on each print for matting and framing, doing all the work myself, making the total cost $75 per print. All three pieces were accepted, and I sold one piece. But there was a price to pay for being successful, because the art organization charged a 20 percent fee for handling the sale. That meant that I went home with $60. It all sounds good and even fair. But think again: if you take off the entry fee of $10 and the money I spent on the materials for the frame, I am now left with $15. The original print for $40 was sold, as far as I was concerned, for $15. Being successful in this case meant that I lost $25. It is a good thing some of us do not have to depend for our living on making and selling art. In any case I learned to watch out and price my work accordingly.

Competitions were important, though, because they allowed me to create a name for myself, which meant that gallery owners and directors paid attention to who I was and what I could do. Commercial gallery

That Glorious Form . . .
forsook the courts of
everlasting day and chose
with us a house of mortal
clay . . . , *1968, color
woodcut, 36″ diameter*

directors contacted me after I won awards. In some cases exhibitions followed a competition. I know that one museum invites the top prize winner to have a solo show the following year. At other times I was asked to participate in group invitational shows, because I had previously received an award. Competitions therefore can be helpful and supportive, but they can also be frustrating, for you do not succeed with every show. I received lots of rejection slips over the years. It still annoys me when that happens. I would, nevertheless, urge you to participate as a way to begin building a solid reputation as a producing artist.

Galleries

The prints that I produced in the late sixties and early seventies were popular, and I had several gallery connections at that time, including a print gallery in Ann Arbor called the Lantern Gallery. Galleries are both fascinating and frustrating places, and the owners can at times be fickle. Many of them want exclusive rights to sell your work. This means that no other gallery can handle your work in a given area. Sometimes a radius of fifty or a hundred miles is established for that purpose. I had an agreement with the Lantern Gallery, and I tried to honor that agreement, but it just so happened that Forsyth Gallery, also located in Ann Arbor, was decorating an entire building in Grand Rapids using Michigan artists. Forsyth Gallery came directly to me to purchase a number of works for the Grand Rapids building. These purchases, made in Grand Rapids, were allowed, for it was well outside the established area. But someone from the Lantern Gallery saw my work at the Forsyth Gallery and reported it to the Lantern Gallery director. She immediately called me and began to accuse me of breaking the contract. I attempted to explain to her what had happened, that the work was there for only one reason, to be framed for the Grand Rapids building. But she would not accept that explanation. There was only one thing left to do. Greta and I drove over to the gallery and picked up our work. When trust is broken, either by the director or by the artist, even

Formation, *1977, acrylic on canvas, 36″ × 48″*

if it is only a misunderstanding, you can not go on as though nothing has happened. Failing to regain the trust left me with only one alternative — to pick up my work and move on.

So I have learned to be careful with gallery owners. They need you and you need them. It is essential that you have a good working relationship with the gallery owner, who is your official representative to the public, and you need to be able to trust that person with everything that you stand for; in turn, the owner needs to be able to count on you that you will continue to produce good solid work that will sell. Trust is a marvelous thing, and you need to nurture and develop and even strengthen it, but that does not mean that you should not have a written business agreement with the director or gallery owner. You need to put everything in writing. If I leave any work behind anywhere — galleries, museums, or even with individuals — I request something in writing. If I have something in writing, it will be clear to everyone what I have agreed on with that person before I leave the place, so that I know the conditions under which I have left my works behind. (In Appendix C I have included a copy of an actual contract that I have used.)

The major gallery director I was dealing with always wanted to raise the prices of my work. But each time we did so, it took me further away from the art market in Grand Rapids. What was reasonable in Chicago or Denver was too high for Grand Rapids or Oklahoma City. I was represented in each of these cities for different periods of time. The same was true for some of the galleries in Canada. Occasionally a gallery owner will suggest that you do more of this, or more of that, because particular works sold more easily. Each case is different, and I therefore do not want to recommend anything other than to advise you to keep your own counsel. There is nothing wrong with trying to find a place for yourself in the art world, but be careful with trying to find a place for yourself in the art market. The market is fickle, and you may never read it quite right, in which case you may have wasted valuable time. I have found it valuable to be informed. Visiting galleries is a way of exploring and collecting information, so that I know what is available,

Terminus, *1968, woodcut,*
36″ diameter

what is selling, and what the current market consists of. If something fits my interest, I go ahead and do it; if not, I say no and move on.

Productivity

The house we bought in Grand Rapids had an extra building in the back. In the summer of 1966, with my father's help, I remodeled the building and made it into a studio. I have found it essential to have a place, even if it is only a corner somewhere, to do my artwork — a private place to consider, play, and produce, but also a place I can walk away from and leave things as they are at that moment. The first artworks produced in the new studio were color woodcut prints. I was limited to this medium because I did not have a press; neither did Calvin College or any other college in the Grand Rapids area in 1966 and '67. After about two years I was able to purchase my own etching press, and as a result I was able to broaden my print production well into the seventies.

I found it difficult, and at times impossible, to balance the various challenges facing me: a young growing family of four children, church, teaching, college committees, establishing an exhibition program at the college, producing my own work, and retaining an active exhibition agenda for myself. If I concentrated on one, all the others would usually suffer. I learned to survive. My art production was neither consistent nor steady. Being a part-time artist is frustrating, but frustration is common for many in the academic world. It was important for me to recognize that the scholar and the researcher were facing the same problem I was facing as an artist. Following a schedule did it for me some of the time; most of the time other demands played havoc with that schedule. Looking back now, I would say that the discipline of working during those scheduled hours was the most important ingredient in my survival as a young artist.

After I began teaching at Calvin College in 1966, I remained active as a graphic designer and as an artist. As a designer I served the college by creating ads, brochures, and pamphlets that would inform the public. Our advertising schedule and budget were very limited in those days, and I could easily maintain the workload in the summer months. I was also responsible for the layout and design of the DIS *Magazine* published by the Dutch Immigrant Society. All of these allowed me to stay in touch with the design field and the printing industry. Preparation and printing were still being done in the same way as when I was a full-time visual designer in Holland, Michigan, in 1962.

As an artist I received my first challenge to serve the college in a special way when Director of College Relations, Sid Youngsma, and President Spoelhof asked me to create a mural for Heritage Hall. There was a beautiful balcony on the second floor that provided a good space for such a mural. They challenged me to create an image that would reflect the heritage of Calvin College and the Reformed tradition. As a recent immigrant I knew nothing about that tradition, so it was easy for me to have an open mind when I began my visual research.

First I searched in the archives at Calvin College; later I found some good material in Holland, Michigan, at the Netherlands Museum. After I read the verbal accounts, I began collecting as many images as I could find. It was important that I understood something of the history before beginning to play with the visual possibilities. Once I understood something of the character of the early immigrants, I made drawings. In these drawings I began to explore various emphases, combining several ideas. Slowly I developed a new appreciation for that peculiar heritage.

After the initial exploratory drawings, I made a final rendering in watercolor and submitted that to William Spoelhof and Sid Youngsma. They both approved the concept and the proposal. The result was an image painted directly on the balcony wall in acrylic paints in the summer of 1967 (see pages 74, 75). It was six feet tall and twenty-eight feet long and took me most of the summer, and over the years was appreciated by the many visitors to Heritage Hall. After I completed the mural, Youngsma talked to me about doing a mural for each dorm. He repeated that request for several years. I said no at the time, for I was not ready to tackle such a big challenge. When Heritage Hall was rebuilt, the balcony wall was saved, but saving the wall was not the answer. For a long time it was in storage, waiting for another place, but it never did find a place elsewhere on our campus. It has now disappeared completely, and I do not know where it went. I learned something from that experience. You do your best, and when the work is done, you must let it go because it is often no longer in your power to control what happens to it. Learn to accept that what was relevant and fitting in one time and place can become irrelevant and unsuitable in another time when other people take over the controls. This was not an easy lesson for me, for no one wants one's work to be set aside or relegated to the past. The truth is that artworks are not always respected in our various communities; in some instances they have even been unintentionally altered to fit other purposes.

Painting the mural Het Woord *in Heritage Hall, Calvin College, summer of 1967*

An example of such an alteration is a piece of sculpture that belonged to a school. It was a painted work of sculpture, and one day someone from the school decided to have the sculpture repainted in the school colors to give it greater identity with the school. The artist was not contacted, and when he discovered what happened, he took the school to court and won the case. The work is now painted again in the original colors. Owning a work of art means that you respect the original work as well as the artist.

In 1968, eleven years after my departure, I returned to the Netherlands with a wife, a daughter, and a three-month-old son. It was a good trip for the whole family. Greta and I have many relatives in the Netherlands and all of them wanted to see us. It was good to be back and see the old places, sleep in the room again where I slept as a teenager, to walk the streets of our village, to worship in the old church my grandfather had helped to build. Above all, it was good to discover how bi-cultural I had become; I was at home in Rotterdam, and twenty-four hours later I was at home in Grand Rapids again. Each place was home, each place familiar and comfortable. The language and the customs allowed me to participate freely in the two different cultures. The trip was less successful for me as an artist; there was neither a place nor a time to work, and little time was left for museums.

The following year we drove west to Vancouver to visit Greta's brothers and sister. The mountains were stupendous; my sense of space was denied. I was closed in, and the grandeur rising in front of me was too overwhelming to capture on any paper. I did some drawings in pencil, combining images that I saw in my rear-view mirror and the winding road in front of me. Recording a mountain is easy; expressing anything beyond that is impossible for me. But we loved the pebbles we found in the mountain streams and rivers and collected many of them.

Focusing on a Theme

Upon my return to the studio I began to draw and paint images of these pebbles, exploring the complexity of the textures, the shapes, and the colors, which are intensified when you wet them. In 1968, both the student painting studio and my office were located on the lower level of the Science Building on the Calvin campus. This provided me with an opportunity to discover a whole new world. Many of the scientists shared with me their sense of wonder about what they studied in their laboratories. Clarence Menninga, a geologist, showed me slices of rocks and how polarized light revealed the inner details of the pebbles I had collected. That new world led to many drawings, prints, and paintings of internal rock structures. For seven years I pursued the rock theme, exploring its symbolism, complexity, and variety. Exploring a theme has allowed me to dig deeper and connect a variety of related ideas. When I suggest to my students that they follow this approach to exploring a theme, many express a fear of repetition, of getting into a rut. Their fear is unfounded, for I have discovered that it is impossible to repeat myself unless I know exactly what I am doing and know in advance what the outcome will be. Assurance of outcome is not the creative act. Moreover, on numerous occasions I have told my students that if they could tell me exactly what they were going to paint, there would be no need to paint it. The act of painting should remain a mystery, an act of exploration, instead of repeating what is already known. Exploring a theme should be an exciting journey of learning and discovering things we had not thought about before.

In 1975 the Dutch Immigrant Society (DIS) approached me to create a number of paintings that would celebrate the Dutch contributions to American culture in connection with the Bicentennial of the U.S.A. I was excited about this project, for it would allow me to show how the Dutch culture had contributed to the American culture in positive and meaningful ways. The Dutch immigrants did not have a positive image of themselves in Grand Rapids, for they knew little about Dutch culture and even less about Dutch culture in the United States. The fact that there had been a Holland-mania in the 1920s, for example, was not commonly known here. Several concepts were discussed, and in the end we decided to make four paintings, each 36″ × 48″ in size, which would show the historical progression beginning with Pieter Stuyvesant, the first governor of New Amsterdam, later to be called New York City, and ending with astronaut Jack Lousma. The research for this project was extensive. The puzzle of fitting all of it into four paintings was a real challenge since it would involve realistic portraits of dozens of people. I relied on my graphic art experience and made several rough layouts to establish the flow and design of each painting. The initial sketches were enlarged, and more and more details were added, until I was sure it would all work. When I was sure that the whole thing was working, I would make a full-value drawing of the entire painting. This drawing was presented for

Twelve Stones, *1975, acrylic on canvas, 36″ × 48″ (Collection of Mr. and Mrs. Conrad Bradshaw)*

In the Oval Office with
President Ford on
February 2, 1976, discussing
the Bicentennial paintings

approval to the committee. After gaining approval, I was free to complete the painting. By the end of 1975 the paintings were finished and framed. On February 2, 1976, a delegation from DIS — William Turkenburg, president; Lucas De Vries, secretary; and Greta and myself — presented the four paintings to President Gerald Ford in the Oval Office of the White House. The President showed much interest and asked several questions about the works and discussed a number of people portrayed in the paintings. Producing these historic works allowed me to make a unique contribution to the immigrant community, for these works directed them to their Dutch-American heroes. My friend Cornelius Barendrecht wrote articles for the Dutch Immigrant Society magazine, describing the paintings and telling the various stories. As a result of our combined efforts, many people, both inside and outside the Dutch immigrant community, now knew about these heroes. This project also illustrated for me how art can be a way of connecting people with each other.

Study of the Dutch Masters

In 1976 I applied for a sabbatical leave of absence. Up to now no one had ever requested time off for a studio project. I did not want to risk being rejected because of the nature of the application. I played it safe and proposed to study the work of the nineteenth-century landscape painters in the Netherlands. The study of these paintings would provide me with a broader background for understanding the work of two major Dutch artists: Vincent van Gogh and Piet Mondrian. The study also required that we move to the Netherlands for eight months with our family of four children, ranging in age from 4 to 11 years. This move would also provide an opportunity to spend time with my immediate as well as with Greta's extended family living in the Netherlands.

My sabbatical study proposal was not only approved by Calvin College but also underwritten partly by the DIS. The Dutch Embassy in Washington, D.C., and the Ministry of Culture in the Netherlands also approved the project. This allowed me free access to all of the major museums and galleries, including their storage areas. Studying and reflecting on the actual works of nineteenth-century landscape painters was a real adventure. Subtle nuances, use of paint, relationships of colors, employment of compositional devices all became clear, because I was looking at the real thing. Seeing these works and reading about these masters was an inspiration to me.

One day I came across this statement by J. H. Weissenbruch: "Our old

Our children in 1979, left to right: Pete, Sonja, Paul, and Joy

masters, more than anyone, taught me how to look at nature. But, of course, nature itself taught me most" (Jacobs, 53). Then I realized what I wanted to do with the rest of my time: I wanted to return to the landscape of my birthplace. As a result I began to look at the landscape with new eyes and a new perspective. The landscape in the Netherlands varies a great deal: from the dunescapes and seascapes along the west coast, to the panoramic polder landscapes of the provinces of Holland; from the gently rolling wooded hills of the eastern part of the country, to the distant views of the wide delta rivers that dissect the land from east to west. We were living in the eastern part, surrounded by woods and farmland. I set up my own small studio in the house we were renting and began the process of rediscovering the Dutch landscape. Watercolor is an excellent medium to use when you are traveling, because it is quick and easy to take along. But in this case I had not planned on doing watercolors and therefore had not taken along any supplies or materials. This was going to be an art history project, so I had not anticipated doing both. With the help of my sisters and brothers, we located some art supply dealers. With the help of my brother-in-law Jitze van der Vinne, I borrowed a large table from a local school. I bought what I needed to begin, experimented with different papers, and began to learn again what it was like to paint in watercolor. At the outset I was not at all sure of what I

Plowed Fields Near
Rotterdam, The
Netherlands, *1978,
watercolor, 20″ × 30″*

Near Lekkerkerk,
the Netherlands, *1978*,
watercolor, 22″ × 30″

wanted to accomplish. But as I progressed, I learned to appreciate anew the spontaneous qualities this medium demands, and eventually I learned something about that peculiar landscape. The first watercolors were rather stiff and concerned only with what the surrounding landscape looked like. The landscape was dominated by trees, with sections of meadows.

We were living in the small rural community of Den Ham. For my art history studies, I needed to travel west for about two hours to get to the major museums, libraries, and art history institutes in The Hague, Amsterdam, Rotterdam, or some other city. On Monday morning I would drive west, depending on where I had scheduled a visit. At the end of the day I would drive to Kralingsche Veer, a small town just east of Rotterdam, to visit with my parents. On Tuesdays and Wednesdays I would return to my studies and appointments, each night returning to my parents to stay and visit. On Thursdays I would return to Den Ham and stay home for ten days to study and to work.

These travels broadened my interest in the Dutch landscape. As a youth I had played in the polder. This is where I grew up. So it was no surprise that the wide polder landscapes began to have a special appeal to me. However, stopping on a major road in Holland is almost impossible except in designated spots, and these spots often would not have the desired view. Therefore I began to record in small drawings what I saw in the polder and along the highways. These small drawings helped me remember and digest what I saw. By using this method, I was able to recall only the major components of the landscape. I slowly became more proficient and gained the freedom necessary to capture those special moments of light, space, and atmosphere that are so characteristic of this land of mist and manure. It took me a couple of months of experimentation to make it work for me. Watercolor often, though not always, requires a quick, spontaneous response. I compare it to running the 100-meter race in track and field sports. It takes a great deal of concentration and preparation, but once that pistol goes off, you go as fast as you can, letting it all out. The time and distance from the scene allowed me to be free and less concerned with all the little details. It forced me to simplify and capture the essence. I was able to complete almost eighty paintings this way. Looking back, it was good to find a way that worked for me, a way that changed from a very tight technique to a very loose approach. I found it by working and in the process discovered the content of this series. It enabled me to discover new dimensions of the old familiar landscape, and as a result I captured something that was precious to me.

Mental concentration and even some kind of ritual preparation were part of my working habits at this time. There was a time for painting, a time for reading and studying, and a time for visiting and playing with the kids. There was a rhythm to our lives that made it free and yet disciplined, open yet planned. My visits to the museum were sometimes like that too. I would walk in and look at only one work, spend ten to fifteen minutes with just that work, and then I would walk out again. The result was that I would remember that painting for a long time. In addition I would make a 3″ × 5″ card for every painting I saw. On that card I would make a small drawing of the work, about 1″ × 2″, and I would record the title, size, date of the work, the name and dates of the artist, and the location. That system allowed me to increase my memory of these works, especially if I could find some readings related to the work or the artist.

The sabbatical study of the nineteenth-century masters taught me many things. I began to appreciate the backgrounds of two major painters in a new way: Vincent van Gogh and Piet Mondrian. Both had their roots in the works of the previous masters. I also developed a personal appreciation for what they were attempting to do with landscape painting. The clouds, the atmosphere, the space, the light are all different in the Netherlands. Something happens to the atmosphere above this waterlogged land, divided by rivers, ditches, canals, lakes, and ponds. Pregnant rain clouds hang above the land, forever battling with an elusive sun, creating a unique gray water wonderland. These nineteenth-century masters responded to that peculiar,

Fields Near Vriezeveen,
the Netherlands, *1978,
watercolor, 22″ × 30″*

Eerde Woods, the
Netherlands, *1978, watercolor,
22″ × 30″ (Collection of
Dr. Schulte Nordholt, The
Netherlands)*

atmospheric landscape, and the watercolors I created reflected a similar interest. In the entry hall of the "Haagse Gemeente Museum" (The Hague City Museum), you will find these words: "EER HET GOD'LIJK LICHT IN DE OPENBARINGEN VAN DE KUNST" (Honor the Godly Light in the Revelations of Art). As a Christian artist I not only appreciated that sentiment, I wanted to reflect it in the work I was doing. The combination of an art history project with a studio project worked well for me, even if that was not the intention originally.

When I returned to Grand Rapids I had three things: an extensive report, a proposal for a nineteenth-century landscape painting exhibition, and a series of watercolors. The report was shared with the administration and the Art Department faculty. The exhibition proposal, however, was not received with great enthusiasm. The Grand Rapids Art Museum had changed directors, and the new director was less interested in a Dutch exhibit and did not want to honor the prior commitments made to me. Funds were also a problem. Later I presented a lecture on my studies at the first meeting of the Historians of Netherlandic Art in Memphis, Tennessee, and became a founding member of that organization. My findings were well received there and were especially appreciated by the Van Gogh and Mondrian scholars. They had known little about these other nineteenth-century Dutch masters. I also presented a major lecture for CIVA, Christians in the Visual Arts, which met at Bethel College in Minneapolis, in 1978, on the experience of returning to my native land. The watercolors I had created in the Netherlands were shown in several exhibitions and were well received. The first was a solo show at Hefner's Art Gallery in Grand Rapids. The Fall Art Faculty Show at Calvin also included many of these works. In 1979 the Forsyth Gallery in Ann Arbor also exhibited the works. This show was highly successful in terms of good reviews and a good number of sales. Remaining works were shown in 1980 in Grand Haven, Michigan, at the Community Center. In 1982 the Vela Gallery in Memphis, Tennessee, displayed some of the Dutch works when I presented my art history project at the University of Tennessee. In the end it was apparent that I had learned more by doing than by studying works of art or reading books about art. The sabbatical project had allowed me to gain a new appreciation for myself as an artist.

Cultural Involvements

College commitments prevented me from doing much art for the next four years. I served on the Board of the Grand Rapids Art Museum, was a member of the Municipal Arts Advisory Commission, the Grand Rapids Arts Council, and several advisory panels of the Michigan Council for the Arts, as well as serving as Chairman of the Art Department. I paid my dues to the community as an artist because I believed that all of us, including artists, need to work on improving the cultural environment so that artists will be more readily accepted and their work more fully appreciated. It is one thing to complain about the isolation of the artist; it is another thing to change it and work for a better relationship. It is in that light that I committed myself to becoming Director of "Connections: A Baroque Festival Year" in 1982. The purpose of the festival was to relate Baroque forms, concepts, ideas, and patterns to the aesthetic, philosophical, theological, and scientific theories of the Baroque period; and to make the Baroque heritage available to our contemporaries so that all of us, seeing the implications and strengths of the Baroque, might help to enliven, revitalize, and even inspirit our own culture. Many people became involved with the project, including faculty and staff from other colleges and universities and two of the major cultural organizations in Grand Rapids: the Polish Heritage Society and the Dutch Immigrant Society. The festival year activities in the West Michigan area included over one hundred events related to the Baroque. It was highly exciting and invigorating. The opening event at the De Vos Hall was televised twice. All the major cultural institutions (the Grand Rapids Symphony, Civic Theater, Opera Grand Rapids, the Grand Rapids Ballet Company, the International Folk Dance Company) and many individuals participated. Bringing together all the arts through a common theme was a new experience for Grand Rapids. Stanley Wiersma, from the English Department at Calvin College, wrote the unifying script for the opening event.

Stanley Wiersma was a leader among young writers and served on the board of the publication *For the Time Being.* This fine arts magazine was published by the Fine Arts Fellowship, a group of writers, composers, poets, painters, and printmakers. Cor W. Barendrecht was the editor, and I worked with Cor as the graphic designer. Cor had collaborated with me on several projects before, especially in connection with a weekly paper from Canada called *Calvinist Contact* and a youth magazine called *Credo.* Sometimes he would write a poem and I would illustrate it; at other times he would write a poem or an article in response to a work I had done. Together we produced several broadsides. The Fine Arts Fellowship would organize annual conferences, promoting dialogue among all the arts. These years of mutual support and interest were vital to my survival as an artist. My involvement with "Connections: A Baroque Festival Year" was a similar adventure; it provided me with an opportunity to learn from others within the academy and the various arts and cultural institutions.

The Baroque Festival Year 1982/83 logo

New Commissions

When the LaGrave Avenue Christian Reformed Church came to me and asked me to do some paintings to help celebrate their hundredth anniversary, I accepted this special challenge and as a result digressed for a short time from landscape painting. Rev. Eppinga had written a book in which he connected each of the pastors with the major cultural events that had taken place during their service at LaGrave Church. After several meetings with the entire committee, the aims and ideas of the project were clarified and defined. Once that was done, I could define the visual direction. Layouts were done and a proposal was written to show how we should proceed. In the proposal I defined the responsibility of the committee in terms of how they would participate and what they would approve. It also specified what kind of freedom I would have to complete the works without being questioned afterwards. There would be ten paintings, one for each pastor. Each painting would include the pastor's wife and images of the major cultural events as described in the book. The committee would help with the research and the selection of the events to be included. Once there was agreement about the selection, I would do a full-scale drawing in pencil to show how all the various parts would fit together. The committee would review the drawing, and after they approved the drawing, I would be free to complete the painting, using the drawing as a guide. The committee was thus directly involved in the process, but not in the final product. In previous cases I had been asked, "Can you not add this, or remove that?" I wanted to avoid such a situation, in which someone would second-guess me after the work was done. Dividing the responsibility this way was accepted and written up in contract form. It proved to be a good working method for the committee and myself. (See Appendix D for a copy of this agreement.)

Another commission, many years later, was for a large landscape painting in an atrium-like lobby. This commission was more straightforward, for it had a space and an idea that were predicated on my previous landscape work. In this instance the client knew what he wanted, knew what I did, and on that basis awarded me the commission. After establishing the size, I made a simple quick drawing of what I wanted to do. Once the drawing was accepted and the work agreed upon, I had complete freedom to finish the commission. I believe the client visited my studio once to check on the progress of the work.

Artist in Residence
After the completion of the Baroque Festival Year, I proposed a sabbatical study that was different in many ways. All the work I had done for the community had taken me away from what I really wanted to do and that

*One of the LaGrave Avenue
Christian Reformed Church
Centennial paintings, 1987,
oil on canvas, 24″ × 24″*

was to spend time in the studio. I had no desire at this time to leave town. The family was growing up and the children were at an age that made it problematic for them to leave school and be out of town. I therefore proposed to be the first Artist in Residence at Calvin College. Some creative figuring allowed me to teach one studio course per semester, one interim course, and one course in the second semester. The rest of the time I would work in the studio producing woodcut prints on the theme of the prophets, priests, and kings, and making large oil paintings of the Midwest. I had no idea where the paintings would take me, for I had never done large works before and neither did I know what kinds of Old Testament characters I would find. The proposal, however, was clear about how I would do this and what I intended to explore. I was therefore pleased when the proposal was approved. I was also a bit surprised, for this was the first time an art project in any discipline was approved. It took some time and effort to find a space, but eventually the college built a studio for me in the Art Department. I was on the way to becoming the first Calvin College Artist in Residence. Two days a week, for three hours, I was available to the public to answer questions or discuss the works I had made. For the rest of the time I was free to work alone in the studio each day.

Questions haunted me when I first moved into the big studio space. I had serious doubts about my ability to sustain a year-long studio effort. Did I still have what it takes after so many years of studio inactivity? Several things happened that prepared me to start working. A solo exhibition at Adrian College in the fall of 1984 provided me with an opportunity to see what I had done so far. It was a kind of retrospective exhibition that allowed me to reflect back on what interested me visually and project forward possible future images I could work on. In the summer of 1984 my sister Nel and her husband Jitze van der Vinne visited us from the Netherlands, and in talking together we vividly recalled the experiences of my 1978 sabbatical year. Nel and Jitze lived only five kilometers (three miles) from us in 1978. All of the previous Dutch studies in which light, space, and atmosphere

Clouds Near Adrian, Michigan, *1985, oil on canvas, 36″ × 60″*

were so dominant made me look up again at the sky. A new expectation grew in me during our summer travels with Nel and Jitze. It became clear that I would make large paintings of the Midwest in which the sky would dominate. These new works would not be unlike my Dutch watercolor paintings done in 1978. Fluffy clouds as well as wild cloud formations, storms as well as gray days would be explored. Previous travels with our own family had taken us all the way to Vancouver, British Columbia, and back. In the course of those travels I had discovered that the wide-open spaces of the prairie intrigued me. That kind of open panoramic space is rare in Michigan. Too many trees, telephone poles, and billboards obstruct our vision. But when you look, you can find some openings even around Grand Rapids. I wanted to take my vague ideas about space, light, and atmosphere and apply them to the mid-western landscape. What I was not ready for was the response of the people who saw these first works in the studio, for they referred to the works as having Dutch skies. These were not Dutch skies; they were studies of clouds I had seen only in Michigan. Dutch skies are different. But I recognized the fact that these were skies seen through Dutch eyes. These space-scapes, as Nick Wolterstorff would call them later, were informed by my studies of the nineteenth-century Dutch landscape painters and by my previous works done in the Netherlands in 1978.

I gradually increased the size of the works from the first painting, which was a modest 36″× 60″, to the last one, which was 66″× 120″. Later I did a triptych that measured 66″× 234″.

It was good for me to work on both the paintings and the prints. The prints required more research, because I did not know much about many of the biblical characters. I found the Jewish writers to be insightful in that regard. They often viewed the prophets, priests, and kings with more empathy and greater appreciation than was shown by other scholars. It may sound strange to do large paintings one day and relatively small woodcuts the next, but I enjoyed the challenge that each provided, and doing the prints allowed me to reflect on things differently. The studio space was large enough to display all the woodcut prints on one wall and four or five large paintings on the rest of the walls. To have the works on display allowed me to reflect on them. I would see things I had not seen before or would catch an idea I had not previously considered. It is important to provide a distance from the work, and to have time to see it with fresh eyes so that your mind can be open to what it really looks like. As a result, some paintings were revisited again and again in order to achieve the desired image. Working on the prints and the paintings provided me with a good balance. It was a good working rhythm. The prints varied in size: the priests were done 20″ square, the kings in a rectangle of 16″× 24″, and the prophets in a 22″ circle.

In the beginning of the year I had resigned from all the committees and boards I was serving on, both for the college and in the community. Now I could work as an artist, free from other commitments, to do what I had set

out to do. To be working full time every day, without interruptions, without meetings, without any other responsibilities except at home was a joy and a pleasure. At the end of the Artist-in-Residence year I was able to mount an exhibition. The Art Department scheduled a show for the spring of 1986. The exhibit was accompanied by a catalog called *Twenty-Five Years as an American Artist,* for which Nick Wolterstorff wrote an introduction. The Sabbatical Exhibition was installed in the Center Art Gallery at Calvin College. Retrospective I was installed at De Graaf Forsyth Galleries in Holland, Michigan, and Retrospective II was installed at De Graaf Fine Arts in Chicago. The exhibits were well received. I felt confirmed in my work as an artist and as a Christian.

The Artist-in-Residency idea led the department and the college to recognize more fully the need to have a studio space available for all of the studio artists, so that students could see how and when we worked. My

Mid West Summer, 1985, oil on canvas, 66″ × 120″

recommendation was that we have separate spaces, one for an office and one for a studio, which is what I had that year. Later when the department remodeled its space, I received a large combined space for both studio and office. I produced many more landscapes and some woodcuts in that new office/studio space.

Integrating the Arts

One of the first prints made during the sabbatical project was reproduced in *Calvinalia,* a flyer that was sent to all Christian Reformed Church families. A Canadian poet, Martin Oordt, who was a Calvin graduate and a teacher of creative writing at the University of Lethbridge in Alberta, saw the small reproduction and responded by writing a rather long poem, which he sent to me. It was a lovely surprise to receive this excellent poem, and I encouraged him to do more. In February of 1985, he attended Calvin's homecoming celebration with his wife Mary, and that is where we met for the first time. Meeting him was a delightful experience. From the moment we first met, there was a deep sense of trust, openness, and support for each other. After seeing all my other works, he took home slides of the

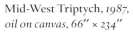

Mid-West Triptych, *1987,*
oil on canvas, 66″ × 234″

prints and of the paintings. He wanted to do more writing in connection with these works. I was delighted and honored. He had collaborated with other artists before, and I too had worked with poets such as Cor W. Barendrecht and Stanley Wiersma before. We were both excited about the possibilities. The poems connected with the prints varied in style and length, and those related to the large paintings were written in haiku, a Japanese poetic form using only seventeen syllables. When Martin's colleague, Dean Blair, received a commission to write a choral work, he came to Martin. Martin in turn gave him the slides and the haiku poetry of the paintings. This sequential series of events led to a première performance by the Alberta Honors Choir of the work called "Cloud Paintings." I was invited to attend this performance in Calgary, Alberta, along with Martin Oordt and Dean Blair. We were all officially recognized that evening. During this performance I projected slides of the works on a large screen while the choir sang. The University of Lethbridge organized a symposium in connection with the project, and as participants we reflected on the sequential nature of the choral work. We expressed the desire to someday do a project together when all of us could start at the same time. Each one of us would

Aaron: One Scapegoat
for All . . . , *woodcut, 20″*
× 20″(above);
Moses: Was Called,
woodcut, 84″ diameter
(right)

Hezekiah: A Measure
of Shadow, *woodcut,*
16″ × 24″

Skyscape near Shelby, Michigan, *1985, oil on canvas, 72″ × 60″*

Lake Effect, *1986, oil on canvas, 66″ × 84″ (Collection of Reformed Bible College, Grand Rapids, Michigan)*

Sunday Morning, *1986,*
oil on canvas, 66″ × 96″

contribute a unique work related to a theme in a given time period without knowing what the other was doing. We enjoyed working together, respecting and appreciating each contribution to the whole project. This experience revealed once again that the Lord works in strange ways. The Lord had put us in contact with each other, which in turn gave us a new sense of purpose. None of us could have anticipated ahead of time how this would come about. Later I would extend a special invitation to Martin Oordt and Dean Blair to cooperate on a prairie project.

A History Project

History projects, like the Heritage Hall mural, the DIS bicentennial paintings, and the LaGrave Church paintings, have always intrigued me. It is a way of keeping stories alive, of encouraging others to tell their story — because when they do, they will tell God's story as well. The residence halls at Calvin College are all named for that reason after famous individuals who contributed of themselves to our denomination and our college. They are our heroes of faith. But the stories of these heroes of faith were not always told, and as a result the students living in these halls were ignorant of the personal histories of these people. In 1988 I proposed to tell the story of those individuals in verbal and visual form. The college awarded me a Faculty Research Fellowship and provided funds to begin the implementation of the project.

Officially I was commissioned by the Student Affairs Division of the college to "research, design, and depict in separate paintings that would colorfully and creatively commemorate these lives and would be hung in the lobbies of these halls." Financial support for this project came from the Residence Life Fund and the Calvin Research Fellowship awarded by the college through its Professional Status Committee.

In January of 1990 the initial research led to the first of fifteen paintings. After two and a half years the entire project was completed. Of the sixteen individuals honored in the fifteen paintings, seven were actually born in the

Netherlands. The process of research and planning was similar to what I had employed in the LaGrave CRC project, for I envisioned a collage-like effect so that many memorabilia could be incorporated into the painting. Each painting was 36″ × 48″. I would make smaller initial drawings to plan each work. After that I would make a drawing the same size as the painting. Using a copy machine, I would reduce or enlarge old photos and materials and paste them in position. This allowed me the freedom to move things around and compose the final image more carefully. When that collage-like drawing was complete and I was satisfied, I would make an outline drawing of all the stuff. This drawing was then traced, and the tracing was carefully transferred to the prepared canvas. The canvas was previously mounted on marine plywood and strengthened with braces in the back and covered with gesso. After the transfer was done, I began the painting. Each section was painted carefully, sometimes aided by the object or by an actual photograph to record each detail as accurately as possible. Oil painting was an excellent medium for this project. The paint can be reduced with oils and varnishes so that it flows more easily from the brush, making it ideal for fine detail. It can also be thinned to be almost transparent, so that it can be used for glazing. On these paintings I used a painting medium called liquin, which is made from an alkyd resin. This medium made the paints dry faster, and is excellent for rendering fine detail as well as for glazing. Collecting and sorting all the various visual materials was a major portion of this project. I could not have done this without the assistance of the people in Heritage Hall and the cooperation of many of the surviving family members. This truly became a community project, for everyone contributed, loaned, or shared in the process. Each of the paintings has now been installed in the appropriate residence hall lobby, along with the identification of the memorabilia. A booklet called *Stories of Faith: Fifteen Heroes of Calvin College and the Christian Reformed Church* was published by the college in connection with this project. The whole experience was very satisfying. The highlight for me personally was the installation of all the paintings in the Center Art

Jacob Noordewier, *1990,*
oil on canvas, 48″ × 60″,
one of the residence hall
paintings

Henry Beets, *1990, oil on
canvas, 48″ × 60″, one of
the residence hall paintings*

Gallery in the Spoelhof Center at Calvin College in the summer of 1992. A reception was held for the surviving family members of those portrayed and for the delegates to the Christian Reformed Church Synod. The fact that the delegates to Synod attended the reception was an indication that the church, too, would claim these heroes of faith. Galen H. Meyer, editor of *The Banner,* a weekly denominational magazine of the Christian Reformed Church, wrote in the foreword:

> When you want to read about the heroes of faith, don't limit yourself to the New Testament letter to the Hebrews. The list there is not complete. Many men and women have since followed the ancient examples of Abraham, Moses, Rahab, Samuel, and the rest who obeyed with single-minded devotion, endured hardship, and kept their eyes fixed on a "better country — a heavenly one." These heroes of a later day have won honored places in the history of the Christian Reformed Church. They have become part of our cherished legacy. (6)

Since the installation of these works in each residence hall, I have been asked numerous times to discuss this project in churches and in the dorms. The future will tell how effective this has been in keeping alive the vision of these heroes.

The Canadian Prairie Project

In 1992, I began to consider a possible focus for my next Sabbatical Leave of Absence. I reflected on the sequential project with the University of Lethbridge faculty and recalled what I had shared with Martin Oordt and Dean Blair. The reciprocal relationship between the creation of paintings, poetry, and then music had been a breath of fresh air for me as an artist. But I also remembered what we had talked about at the symposium. I contacted Martin Oordt to feel him out regarding working together on a prairie-inspired project, and within a few weeks, three faculty members of the University of Lethbridge were committed to collaborating with me on

View from 520 towards
Claresholm, Alberta, *1993,*
drawing, 20″ × 20″

View from 520 towards
Claresholm, Alberta, *1993,*
watercolor, 22″ × 22″

the project: Martin Oordt as poet, Carl Granzow as sculptor, and Dean Blair as composer. All were eager to produce works related to the expansive space and productivity of the Canadian prairie. Our main contact was via e-mail, which provided a marvelous way to bounce ideas around and to define the nature of the project we would work on together. To my delight, Calvin College approved my Sabbatical proposal. Carl Granzow invited me to study the prairie firsthand by becoming the Artist in Residence at the Gushul Studio in Blairmore, a small mining town in the Crowsnest Pass of southern Alberta. The Gushul Studio is owned by the Province of Alberta as a historic landmark and run by the Art Department of the University of Lethbridge. They invited me for two months, and in July and August of 1993 we worked and lived in the Gushul Studio. A Faculty Research Fellowship from the Calvin College Alumni Association supported these months of investigation. During the summer months of 1993, the four of us met on several occasions, either at the Gushul Studio or at the University of Lethbridge.

From left to right: Carl Granzow, Chris Stoffel Overvoorde, Dean Blair, and Martin Oordt

The prairie is an awesome place to me. It is like the ocean in many ways; the uninterrupted view is the same, and so are the gently rolling slopes. As a Dutchman I love space, and I have always been intrigued, just like my mother, with the sky. But the prairie is not at all like the Dutch landscape; it is much more forbidding. The space is more immense and the distances are much greater than you can experience in even the widest polder landscape in the Netherlands. To look for thirty miles and not see more than two farms is unthinkable in the Netherlands, or in Michigan. Not so on the prairie, where the space goes on indefinitely. The space has a quieting effect on me, for it says to me again and again, "The Lord is God, the Lord is One, the Lord is infinite, the Lord is eternal." It is when you stand in a field of grain, and you see nothing else for miles but a faint distant horizon, that you get a new perspective on who you are in relation to nature and how you are related to God. That is why the prairie is quieting but also why I call it awesome, for it reminds me in so many ways of how great God is and how small I am. How strong and powerful the wind can be that he created, how mighty the rain and hailstorms that he can send. How dependent we are upon him for all the things we need. It is all that and much more that motivated me to create these works. If I have captured something of that feeling between quieting and awesome, something of that perspective of space, it is because I have responded to what I saw, to what I experienced. Seeing with the physical eye is not enough; seeing with the spiritual eye is what I was searching for in these drawings, watercolors, and oil paintings. The knowledge that God is the creator of nature — and of me — has affected my perception of nature.

To explore this new space meant that I had to stand with my feet in the soil and experience anew that special relationship a landscape painter has to have with his subject matter. To see a particular place and record in a small sketch some possibility for a larger drawing, a watercolor, or a small oil color study was a way of claiming the place for me. To experience nature is not to experience art. Nature, although marvelous and inspirational, is not a work of art. My experience of nature, no matter how magnificent or intense, needs to be processed into visual images. Artists have the responsibility to respond visually to nature and to the self. When artists combine these two elements, art can become a response that connects insight, emphasis, or viewpoint to a sense of place and provides a sense of belonging for the viewer.

As a landscape painter, I have rediscovered that the character of the place where you work can become a major source of inspiration. Working in the Gushul Studio in the small mining town of Blairmore, Alberta, was a unique experience for me. I was motivated by the light and space of the place from the moment we arrived on June 30, 1993, until the last day,

The Prairie Near Cardston, Alberta, *1993, pencil drawing, 20″ × 20″*

Moon and Clouds Near
Cowley, Alberta, *1994,
oil on canvas, 48″ × 48″*

which was August 29. The north wall is mostly glass and so is part of the ceiling, bathing the studio in daylight. I was truly inspired to produce. During that period I was able to create sixty pencil drawings. These drawings became important to me; they were my way of understanding the relationships of value, proportions, scale, atmosphere, and light. I also produced forty watercolors and forty oil sketches for a total of 140 works. It was the most intense two months of my life as an artist; never before had I produced this many works in such a short period. (See page 69 for a photo of the studio.)

These studies in pencil, watercolor, and oil also became my way of dealing with the complexity of the immense space in which the traditional perspective rules of Western art did not seem to fit. These scribbles on paper became my way of digesting and understanding, my way of exploring and discovering new ways of thinking and working. Once I had done the value drawings, I could begin to explore color combinations that would reflect the reality of what I experienced both physically and spiritually. Collecting all that data was exciting, and that excitement was carried over into the Calvin College studio. I began working on the larger works in the fall of 1993.

The size and scale of the canvas have become important to me over the years. Before I left for Canada that summer, I was working in a square format, and soon after my arrival at the Gushul I adopted the square for the remainder of my studies of the prairie. The square is hard to work in, for it denies the natural horizontal format of the landscape. It was a special challenge to me. It was also something that unnaturally belongs to the prairie because man has taken the expanse of the prairie and superimposed upon its natural contours a subdivision of sections of one square mile. You can find a section road every two miles throughout most of southern Alberta. The square paintings, then, are indicative of an art problem, but they also reflect the history of man's interaction with the prairie. After completing fourteen of the large 48″ × 48″ oil paintings, I considered

Rain in the East, Near
Hillspring, Alberta, *1994,*
diptych, oil on canvas,
48″ × 96″ (Collection of the
Zeeland, Michigan, Library)

expanding the format to double that size. During my second visit to the Gushul Studio and the prairie in the spring of 1994, I became more acutely aware of what I was leaving out by using only the square format. I did several drawings and watercolors of a double square and even some triple squares. During that short visit I was able to meet with Carl Granzow and Martin Oordt several times at the Gushul Studio in Blairmore to check notes, ideas, and progress. That visit was again a refreshing time for me. The challenging discussions we had, combined with being back in the place, inspired me to explore the diptych and the triptych format. Each of us was developing a window peculiar to our respective skills and interests. Seeing the other windows become clearer was helpful in seeing my own.

Virginia Bullock wrote the following about this installation in the catalog:

> The grandeur and awe of one facet of God's vast creation — the prairie — has struck a mutual responsive chord in four of His people. Their worthy attempts to acknowledge their Creator's gift by expressing their own unique disciplines provided . . . four special windows into the prairie for us to savor. (7)

The Prairie Vision project was a collaborative effort. I experienced a deep sense of support, along with all the other participants. As artists we need each other; we need to support each other in the process, no matter what our medium is or our art discipline or our cultural background. Working together and learning from each other, especially across the disciplines, can be enriching beyond words. I highly recommend it for young art students in a college setting where opportunities to share abound. I will say more about that in Chapter 6, "The Artist and the Community."

A Place for Art

Artists do not need to look far to serve others with their artwork. A visual response to our immediate community, its various issues and problems, or its celebrations, can be rewarding in itself. The relationship between the

artists and the community can be enhanced when we as artists participate
in that community. If we fail to be of service to those near, what will we
do with those who are far away? Art needs the human connection, not
only between artists and their work, but also between the work and other
persons. For me a work is not completed until it has found a place. When a
community, however small, has claimed it as being of value and significance
to them, the work has found a place. This can be a home or a church; it can
also be a school, a hospital, a college dining room, or a museum. But if your
work does get into a museum, don't set your hopes too high, for this may
be the best way to have the work placed in storage. Museum collections are
often much larger than their exhibition space. A given museum may work
hard at rotating the showing of its collection, but even then it may be years
before your work is shown in public. For example, in 1965 I did a woodcut-
print called "Forbid Them Not . . . ," which is 36″ × 48″ in size. The Grand
Rapids Art Museum awarded me the Purchase Award in Printmaking in
the Michigan Painters and Printmakers Competition of 1965. I was greatly
honored by that event for two reasons: it was a deeply religious theme,
and it was a woodcut. Both of these were rare occurrences in statewide
competitions. Since that award was made in 1965, the print has been seen
only once — for a period of three weeks in March of 1981 when it was
included in one of the "City Focus" exhibits. Three weeks in over fifteen
years; that's all. The honor this print received placed it in storage and hid
it from view. Under those conditions it is impossible to be meaningful to
a community, any community. Another print from the same edition was
presented to the Oakdale Christian School and is proudly displayed in their
teachers' lounge. Here all the staff and many of the students can see it
every day. Since the original print was motivated by a response to racism,
it is a perfect place for that particular image, for it says that everyone is
welcome in the arms of Jesus whether you are beautiful or ugly, black or
white, smart or academically challenged, a fast runner or a bad basketball
player. Oakdale is a Christian inner-city school, and I am sure that the print

Forbid Them Not . . . ,
1966, woodcut, 36″ × 48″

has been claimed by that community in a special way. All our children went to Oakdale School. Oakdale was part of our regular community, and I was deeply moved and grateful to see that print in that place. So where is honor to be found? Not in the museum, but in the community where your art is accepted and claimed as a meaningful visual image. Serving others means that we are ready to participate and contribute whenever the opportunity comes to us.

Chapter Six

The Artist and the Community

"...so that in all things God may be praised through Jesus Christ."

1 Peter 4:11

The One in the Many, Yet One in Christ

In the previous chapters, "My Initial Journey" and "My Journey as an Artist," I explored the various ways of serving different kinds of communities as a person, as a Christian, as a graphic designer, and as a fine artist.

There are three parts to this chapter. In the first part I want to discuss the mystery of each of us being made differently and yet into one body in Christ. In the second part I wish to explore the role of art and the power it has for us. In the third part I want to discuss ways in which art can successfully function in the church, the community, the school, and the home.

Whenever we talk about art, we want to discuss talent, because artists are known as especially talented in some way. They have received the gift, like the appointment of Bezalel in the story of the tabernacle in Exodus 35:30-35. When we do that, however, we fail to recognize that each of us is different, uniquely created; all of us are endowed with gifts and talents. These gifts and talents set us apart from each other, for none of us have received identical gifts. In 1 Peter 4 we discover the reason why we have different gifts:

> [10]Each one should use whatever gift he has received to serve others, faithfully administering God's grace in various forms. . . . [11]If anyone serves, he should do it with the strength God provides, so that in all things God may be praised through Jesus Christ.

This text implies that we have received the gifts "to serve others." So, being different from each other is not some grand mistake on God's part; it is part of his plan. He intended each of us to be different. What applies to each of us individually also applies to different groups, different tribes, different cultures, and different nations. In Christ we are one, and we may recognize and rejoice in our differences as long as we use our differences to "serve others"; and when we do, we celebrate our oneness in Christ.

The apostle Paul says it even more forcefully in his first letter to the Corinthians, the twelfth chapter, where he elaborates on the interconnectedness of the Christian community. He observes that we are different, each being a different part; yet no part can do without the other.

> [12]The body is a unit, though it is made up of many parts; and though all its parts are many, they form one body. So it is with Christ. [13]For we were all baptized by one Spirit into one body — whether Jews or Greeks, slave or free — and we were all given the one Spirit to drink. [14]Now the body is not made up of one part but of many. [15]If the foot should say, "Because I am not a hand, I do not belong to the body," it would not for that reason cease to be part of the body. [16]And if the ear should say, "Because I am not an eye, I do not belong to the body," it would not for that reason cease to be part of the body. . . .
>
> [21]The eye cannot say to the hand, "I don't need you!" And the head cannot say to the feet, "I don't need you!" [22]On the contrary, those parts of the body that seem to be weaker are indispensable. [24]. . . But God has combined the members

of the body and has given greater honor to the parts that lacked it, [25]so that there should be no division in the body, but that its parts should have equal concern for each other. [26]If one part suffers, every part suffers with it; if one part is honored, every part rejoices with it.

The above verses make it clear that we need each other; no one should stand apart or alone. We were made for each other; we are interdependent in Christ Jesus our Lord. The recognition that we have no control or power over the selection of our gifts and talents is important. For if we have no choice in the matter, we have no reason to boast about what we have received. It is God who gives the gifts and the Lord Jesus who makes us into one. For the artists among us, that means two things. First, the artist should be humble about the gifts that he or she has received from God. There is no need for the artists in our midst to feel special or to develop a superior attitude, acting as though they have some special insight. Second, it means that the artists among us ought to be accepted as fellow believers and recognized as those who can serve and enrich all of us in our lives as Christians. That should be the model for our Christian community.

Each of us is gifted to serve the other. Christ in his servant role becomes the model. Thomas Thompson explores an amazing model in his essay in the book, *The One and the Many: Christian Identity in a Multicultural World*, using the words of the Philippian hymn as found in the book of Philippians, chapter 2 (his translation):

> [6]*Who being in the form of God,*
>   *did not consider equality with God*
>   *something to be grasped (harpagmon),*
> [7]*but he emptied (ekenosen) himself,*
>   *taking the very nature of a servant,*
>   *being made in human likeness.*

Thompson raises this question for us:

> Now if the second Adam (Christ) for the welfare of another crossed the great metaphysical divide between God and humanity, Creator and creature, can we not in imitation of him cross the less essential divides that separate us, to encounter and embrace those who are also created in the very same image? . . . If we in the Christian church are ungraceful about affirming others because we stumble over distinctions of race, ethnicity, or culture, then it is quite possible that we have too tight of a grip on our own lives, a false (i.e., insecure) image of ourselves, which we may have to learn to ungrasp. . . . In imitation of Christ, we are called to empty ourselves. But unlike that One who emptied himself of an all-entitled glory, we must empty ourselves of a vain and empty glory." (23)

Jesus himself puts it this way: "If you cling to your life, you will lose it; but if you give it up for Me, you will save it" (Matt. 10:39, *Living New Testament*).

Christians, and that includes the Christian artists among us, are called to implement this concept in word and deed. We need to begin to recognize that we are diverse for a good reason. The recognition that diversity is natural, that it is intended and is not some grand mistake, is essential for our understanding.

When Calvin College challenged me to become the Director of the Multicultural Year (1995 / 1996), I used it as an opportunity to explore these ideas and put them into practice. Working as the Multicultural Year Committee, we declared that:

> Diversity is nature's common language. From the songs of birds and the patterns of snowflakes to the abundant variety in a bouquet of flowers, God reveals himself by speaking through nature's rich diversity. That same richness is present in the Kingdom of Christ: ". . . a great multitude . . . from every nation, tribe, people and language . . ." (Rev. 7:9). "To be in Christ is to be reconciled with

one another as a community of racially and ethnically diverse people of God" (proposed statement, Christian Reformed Church Synod, 1996).

In our attempt to illustrate this kind of diversity, we adopted a bouquet of flowers as a visual reminder of our need to explore and practice the unity we have in Christ. Calvin College initiated the Multicultural Year in response to the tenth anniversary of the Comprehensive Plan. This plan was intended to increase the minority representation among the staff, the students, and the faculty. The plan for the Multicultural Year was simple: to invite eight different cultural groups to the campus to introduce us to their culture. We needed to be taught, and they needed to be given an opportunity to teach us. This approach was born out of a deep respect, acceptance, and appreciation for each group. As an artist I was convinced that we needed to experience each group's cultural uniqueness. All of us in our respective disciplines had spoken, theorized, planned, and issued statements and declarations. Now it was time to look, smell, taste, listen, and experience each culture. The students on campus were invited to taste and smell the food of a different culture throughout the academic year. The Calvin Food Service once a month presented a special ethnic meal prepared in cooperation with the various ethnic groups.

Multicultural Year Logo

Here are some of the cultural highlights of the Multicultural Year presented on the Calvin College Campus.

In September the exhibition Faith and Hope: The Art of Hispanic Culture (*Fe Y Esperanza: Arte de Cultura de Hispaño*) was installed in the Center Art Gallery, and many Latino speakers were brought in.

In October the Korean committee was able to bring the Seoul Metropolitan Dance Theater to the campus. It was the first time this troop had performed on a college campus.

In November a highly successful Anishinabe Pow Wow was held in the Fieldhouse, with local Native American Nations.

In December the Dearborn Traditional Arabic Ensemble presented a wonderful concert and dance performance by Arabs living in West Michigan.

The Chinese organizations in town cooperated with each other for the first time to present a marvelous celebration of the Chinese New Year.

Concerts and major speakers dominated the month of February when the African American community came to our campus in large numbers. The "Sounds of Blackness" filled the Fine Arts Center Auditorium.

The famous Taburitzans helped us celebrate Eastern European cultures.

Laotians and Cambodians presented another New Year celebration in April.

After all these multicultural experiences, we closed the Multicultural Year with an International Symposium on Christian Diversity. A publication emerged out of that conference called *The One in the Many: Christian Identity in a Multicultural World,* edited by Thomas R. Thompson. The Multicultural Year included well over a hundred activities, from speakers to concerts, from fashion shows to international dance performances, from exhibitions to symposiums — all of it made possible thanks to a generous grant from the Jay and Betty Van Andel Foundation.

What did I do that was so different? First, I went to each group and identified an organization, a church, a clinic, or a service organization that would work with me. The Multicultural Year Committee formed twelve different subcommittees; I chaired nine of them. The idea was to create an open, non-threatening teaching environment, and the first questions we asked were: How do you wish to present your culture? What can we do to facilitate? Who and what do you need to make it possible? The responses varied greatly and the activities that grew out of our deliberations were as different as the cultures we selected. It was rewarding to bring together the various groups and let them tell us what and how they wanted to present their culture to our campus. I look back on my involvement with pleasure, and I am grateful that as an artist I was able to contribute in this way to the academic community. Only when we can trust each other can we begin to learn and experience how others perceive, respond, and express themselves individually and corporately. I attempted to facilitate an educational experience that went beyond the stereotypes and the academic jargon, instead of assuming that we — the academic community — were the greatest source of knowledge, as is often our posture.

When it comes to accepting others from a different culture, we often assume that we have to give up something. It is as though our cultural baskets are full and we cannot get more in unless we throw out something first. But that is not the case; if anything, I have developed a deeper appreciation of my own Dutch heritage by studying and experiencing other cultures. During the Multicultural Year I was enriched beyond measure by my Korean, Native American, Latino, Cambodian, Laotian, Chinese, and Eastern European acquaintances. Regardless of cultural origin, the arts, especially the performing arts, have a way of building bridges of insight and appreciation that reach beyond the academic jargon and theories. The same may be said for the art and culture of different periods, for although we look at the work of the seventeenth-century masters with our twenty-first-century eyes, we can still be informed and even edified by the works of these old masters. When we do, we are not deprived of any of our twenty-first-century notions but rather deepened by the art of a previous century.

The Role and Power of Art

Images are powerful reminders in both the fine arts and popular culture. They are reminders, or connectors, that connect us with aspects of our lives below the surface of things. What is it, for example, that makes Elvis Presley the "King"? Or how do we explain the healing power of the Vietnam Veterans Memorial? It was the result of an open competition of 1400 entries. A jury selected the design of Maya Ying Lin of Athens, Ohio, who in 1980 was a 21-year-old architectural student at Yale University. She proposed two walls, each 246′ 8″ long, angled towards the Lincoln Memorial and the Washington Monument. On these dark granite walls, 59,939 names were grit-blasted in the order in which they were taken from us. That is the description of the wall. Its impact can be experienced only when you view the site of the installation where it becomes a park within a park, a healing wall that has united us in a way that no other expression has been able to do. It revealed the depth of our grief as a nation. "Visual art is a revelation," says Leland Ryken in his introduction to the visual art section of the book *The Christian Imagination.* He goes on to say, "it aims to rescue us from inattentiveness and half awareness — the normal state for most of us" (357). The artists in our midst can lead us, can help us focus, can call us to attention; and the use of our senses requires attention. God is visible through his creation, as has been stated so beautifully in the second article of the Belgic Confession. Artists, both Christian and non-Christian, may reveal, call attention to, testify; make visible what is not known, what is hidden, what is forgotten, what is ignored, what is denied. What separates us from the unbeliever is expressed in the Heidelberg Catechism, Lord's Day 12, question and answer 32:

Q. But why are you called a Christian?

A. Because I am a member of Christ by faith, and thus a partaker of His anointing, that I may confess his name, present myself a living sacrifice of

Isaiah: Misplaced Trust
Shamed, *1985, woodcut,
22″ diameter*

Saul: Obedience Rather Than Strength, *1986, woodcut, 24.5″ × 16″*

thankfulness to Him, and with a free and good conscience fight against sin and the devil in this life, and hereafter reign with Him eternally over all creatures.

The answer alludes to the three offices of the believer: prophet, priest, and king; in Christ we are all three. Artists are no different in that respect from other believers. Some will be prophetic in their work and announce or hint at what is, or what will come, exposing and challenging us to deal with the issues of justice, violence, poverty, and hunger. Others will work on assisting us in worship and as such fulfill a unique role as believers and as priests. Still others will proclaim the royalty of Christ in the glorious works they produce. Some artists will do all three excellently, while others may practice the one more than the other. The artist can function in any combination, for within the Christian community he or she can combine being a prophet with being a priest, building and encouraging, helping to remember, and inviting us to worship and celebrate. Artists may challenge us with a prophetic image or expose the anger of a king, as I did when I created the image of Saul and Samuel, and we may feel uncomfortable in viewing such an image. But in this case we are meant to be uncomfortable, for the story is filled with discomfort. Art can help us confront such discomfort through an image, or it can raise questions and expose our values. Another example is the woodcut "Isaiah: Misplaced Trust Shamed," which illustrates the story of Isaiah: "Then the Lord said: 'Just as my servant Isaiah has gone stripped and barefoot for three years as a sign and portent against Egypt and Cush'" (Isaiah 20:3), because the Israelites had not trusted God but the Egyptians to help them in time of trouble (see page 153). Art has a way of reminding us not only of the good but also of the bad. Art is not always pleasant and comfortable or cozy.

I have talked about New York City, about Andy Warhol and others who dominated the art scene in that city. I recognize as an artist that New York City is an art center, an important place to visit and be enlightened by the marvelous storehouses of art available there. But as an artist I also need to

Trees, 1969, wood engraving (actual size), 1.125″ × 2.5″

recognize that this center is far removed from most of us living in other places. Most of the time it does not concern us, and we are aware of the place only as a cultural center. Do we need such a center in order to be culturally vital? Is New York the place that sets the standards for us as Christians in terms of art and the art market? In graduate school, I, like everyone else, followed closely what was happening in New York. But even at that time, I did not follow up on what I was learning. I followed my own directions and interests, fully aware of the latest trends and happenings. At that time landscape painting and figure painting were not popular, but I wanted to make landscapes because that was my interest. I felt that as a Christian artist I had personal values and concerns that went beyond the latest trends. Some would call these concerns provincial, trite, and old-fashioned, meaning they were narrow and out of date. It would be a mistake, however, to think that New York is broadminded, for the New York establishment has shown again and again how narrow its views of art have been. Landscape painting and figurative works were scorned by the New York critics and the establishment for many years; indeed, New York is still having trouble accepting many kinds of realism.

As a Christian community that includes artists, we can begin to create our own centers, establish our own standards as to how we want to use art in our circles, in our communities, in our congregations. A center has a core, and that core for us should be the church, the local church. But that means greater involvement, increased understanding, and an educational enterprise that will inform the congregation about art in all of its complex dimensions. The cultural dimension of our church today needs revival so that the arts can play a more vital role in the life of the congregation. The dialogue between the artist and congregation needs to start at the local level. If and when it does, it can have a tremendous impact. For example, the Peace Lutheran Church in Sparta, Michigan, which organized the Annual Christian Arts Shows, had a great impact on the cultural scene in western Michigan. Closer to home for me was the unique experience of having Grace Church come to the Center Art Gallery at Calvin College on Palm Sunday, 1986. My large cloud paintings were on display that month, and people wanted to have an opportunity to see them and have me talk about them. Things did not work out that way. Reverend Roger Van Harn held a regular service and preached a sermon that evening in the gallery, using the paintings and prints on display. I never said a word. Even if he had asked me, I am not sure I would have been able to speak, for I was very moved by the entire experience of turning the gallery into a worship space. Van Harn had also written a poem for the occasion:

"You Belong to God"
(For Chris Overvoorde, Grace Church, and God's Glory)

Fields farmed and fenced,
Dressed and kept,
You savor the memory of an ancient Garden.
Fertile and fruitful,
You soothe the fears of a distant city.
Fields formed by Word and work,
Called from chaos,
Born anew by unfailing promise,
Converted by renewing grace,
Justified by working faith,
Sanctified by successive seasons,
Glorified by exalted skies.
Redeemed fields,
Freed for an everlasting covenant
Beyond earth's boundaries,
Signed and sealed
With clear clouds that say:
You belong to God.

Canvas stretched and framed,
Sketched and shaded,
You savor the memory of an ancient story.
Tinted and hued,
You soothe the fears of a pilgrim people.
Canvas formed by Word and work,
Called from chaos,
Born anew by unfailing promise,
Converted by renewing grace,
Justified by working faith,
Sanctified by successive seasons,
Glorified by exalted skies.
Redeemed canvas,
Freed in an everlasting covenant
Beyond gallery walls
Flushed and dyed
With sacramental colors that say:
You belong to God.

Roger Van Harn
Palm Sunday, 1986

I cannot recall another experience that has brought me closer to my fellow believers than what happened that night in the Center Art Gallery. It is a great affirmation and delight when artist and church come together and make beautiful images and music together because we belong to God. We want to celebrate that simple, rich truth — that we belong. This very idea should define our culture, should motivate our responses, and should fill our existence.

The shallowness of our existence, however, even our Christian existence, makes it hard to reclaim or reform, let alone transform our culture in the

Installation of sabbatical exhibition – Center Art Gallery, Calvin College, 1986

name of Christ. Young Christian artists find it hard to endow their work with meaning and insight because their lives are no different from those around them. Our lives are disconnected: what we do does not often reflect what we believe. Secular symbols, from beer ads to cars, are better known to us than the symbols used in our worship spaces. The intensity with which we watch TV is rarely matched in our Sunday morning worship. Moreover, the world has claimed many of the traditional Christian symbols. In times of fire, tornado, or flood, who arrives first? The Red Cross is our first response in many cases; the red cross of the ultimate atonement is now a secular image that assures us in time of need. Like Isaiah's story of the Israelites who trusted in the treaty with Egypt and Cush, we trust in Blue Cross and Blue Shield to help us in time of trouble. It is not because we do not know about images; images are hurled at us faster than ever before. They are ingrained into our being; they influence what we eat for breakfast and how we sleep at night. As a matter of fact, we have been numbed by the endless bombardment of visual images via the electronic media, including the Internet. Because of the popular media, we have an uncritical view of images that are cheap, artificial, drab, and downright ugly. This in turn has led to a sensory indulgence, because we have paid little attention to protecting our sensory life from decay. We have become shallow and superficial in our use of images. And sadly, our religious beliefs and values are seldom expressed in visual form.

This degeneration of the use of images is doubly tragic in my view, for in my lifetime I have seen doors opened to artists, like myself, that were previously closed. The Christian Reformed community has not always been accepting of the artist. Artists, unless they were organists or choir directors, were often allowed rather than accepted. Much of that has changed, and I have been delighted to see a greater acceptance of Christian artists, of their work and contributions, even in worship.

It is my contention, however, that our peculiar Dutch Reformed heritage has yet another problem: it has a fear of the senses — or if not a fear, a strong distrust. One of the possible explanations is that we have confused the terms "sensuous" and "sensual." "Sensuous" means affecting the senses, especially aesthetically, whereas "sensual" refers to physical, sexual pleasure. "Sensuous" ought to be one of the positive words in a Christian's vocabulary, not one of the fearful words. The fear of our senses has disabled our praise and numbed our ability to give thanks. Moreover, giving thanks in our numbed condition may be a problem. How do you give thanks for something you have never noticed? How do you praise God for something you did not see or have not experienced with your senses? We are anxious about many things, many little things, but when Jesus said, "Consider the lilies of the field," he was not making a moralistic statement. He was pointing out that though the lilies were apparently lazy and unproductive, occupying valuable space, they were there for no other reason than to give glory to God. Our business is not to be anxious but to praise God, and we may praise him with our senses. We could and should have access to God through the full use of our senses. It should be our goal to praise him with our whole being, and we should do it with all the intensity, all the concentration and attention we can muster.

Christ himself invites us to do that, for it is hard to exclude our senses from the sacraments. In the sacraments, Christ has given us the water of baptism, the bread and wine of his Holy Supper to eat and drink; he invites us to wash, to taste, to feel, to smell, to see, and to hear. Faith and the senses are intertwined with each other in the sacraments. Jesus used ordinary things like bread, wine, and water to teach us something about his kingdom. Ordinary things from nature are transformed into transcendent reminders.

When it comes to reading the book of nature, mentioned in the second article of the Belgic Confession, we have trouble reading it meaningfully. The Reformed tradition has not been strong in teaching that kind of reading. This in part may be due to a lack of knowledge about the visual images in the Old and New Testament. We are startled when Old Testament scholars tell us that the biblical message has come down to us not only through an analytical/exegetical tradition, but also through an artistic tradition. Many theologians do not know this "artistic tradition" in the Bible. The Old Testament is rich in visual history, as we discovered in the story of Bezalel. I have never found a children's Bible that included the story of Bezalel, nor do I know of any Sunday School material on him. We need to recognize that the tabernacle and all that was part of it, the vessels and the vestments, the tools and the cloth — all of them were reminders that God was present among them. I like to call them visual reminders rather than symbols, for they functioned as a reminder in a visual form, and that is what a symbol really is. There are many stories in which God tells the people of Israel that they should remember this deed or that event. Some reminders were affirmative of God's work; others recalled the sin and disobedience on the part of the people or specific individuals.

When Jacob dreams his dream of angels ascending and descending, he erects a stone so that he will remember the place. In Genesis 28 we read:

> [16]When Jacob awoke from his sleep, he thought, "Surely the Lord is in this place, and I was not aware of it." [17]He was afraid and said, "How awesome is this place! This is no other than the house of God, this is the gate of heaven." [18]Early the next morning Jacob took the stone he had placed under his head and set it up as a pillar and poured oil on top of it. [19]He called that place Bethel. . . .

Jacob's stone pillar was a personal reminder. The reminder in the Valley of Achor is less well known. It is the story of Achan, who says in Joshua 7:

> [21]"When I saw in the plunder a beautiful robe from Babylonia, two hundred shekels of silver and a wedge of gold weighing fifty shekels, I coveted them and took them. They are hidden in the ground inside my tent, with the silver underneath." . . . [24]Then Joshua, together with all Israel, took Achan son of

Zerah, the silver, the robe, the gold wedge, his sons, and daughters, his cattle, donkey and sheep, his tent and all that he had, to the Valley of Achor. ²⁵Joshua said, "Why have you brought this trouble on us? The Lord will bring trouble on you today." Then all Israel stoned him, and after they had stoned the rest, they burned them. ²⁶Over Achan they heaped up a large pile of rocks, which remains to this day. Then the Lord turned from his fierce anger. Therefore that place has been called the Valley of Achor ever since.

This is a visual reminder of God's anger at flagrant disobedience, but it is also a reminder of how he forgives and turns away from his anger. The Israelites had to learn this lesson again and again. Each time, the Lord provided them with a visual reminder, an object lesson. Consider, for example, the account in Numbers 21, where the Israelites rebelled against the Lord in the wilderness:

> ⁴They traveled from Mount Hor along the route to the Red Sea, to go around Edom. But the people grew impatient on the way; ⁵they spoke against God and against Moses, and said, "Why have you brought us up out of Egypt to die in the desert? There is no bread! There is no water! And we detest this miserable food!" ⁶Then the Lord sent venomous snakes among them; they bit the people and many Israelites died. ⁷The people came to Moses and said, "We have sinned when we spoke against the Lord and against you. Pray that the Lord will take the snakes away from us." So Moses prayed for the people. ⁸The Lord said to Moses, "Make a snake and put it up on a pole; anyone who is bitten can look at it and live." ⁹So Moses made a bronze snake and put it upon a pole. Then when anyone was bitten by a snake and looked at the bronze snake, he lived.

This is a powerful image of sin, confession, and redemption in the middle of the desert. God commanded them to see, and in seeing they would live. Jesus himself refers back to this story in John 3:

¹³No one has ever gone into heaven except the one who came from heaven — the Son of Man. ¹⁴Just as Moses lifted up the snake in the desert, so the Son of Man must be lifted up, ¹⁵that everyone who believes in him may have eternal life.

There are many other stories that describe visual reminders of what God has done in the lives of his people. There is the Ark of the Covenant, and the items inside the Ark. The tabernacle itself is later translated into the architectural wonder of King Solomon's temple. It is always God who acts first, and the act is often followed up with an instruction so that we will remember the event, like the story in Joshua 3, which recounts how God led the people of Israel through the river Jordan. Joshua 4 tells the story of the twelve stones:

> ²Take twelve men from the people, from each tribe a man, ³and command them to take twelve stones from here out of the midst of the Jordan, from the very place where the priests' feet stood, and carry them over with you, and lay them down in the place where you lodge tonight.

Twelve stones, insignificant by themselves; they could not have been very big, for they had to be carried to the encampment, which was a couple of miles away. Did they arrange them in a special way to make them unique? How unique were the stones themselves? Twelve stones were to be a visual reminder of what God had done that day. In verse 21 Joshua says something rather interesting:

> ²¹When your children ask their fathers in time to come, what do these stones mean? ²²Then you shall let your children know, "Israel passed over this Jordan on dry ground."

Why would children ask such a question if there was nothing special about them, nothing peculiar? Of course there must have been something

Twelve Stones, *1990,
oil on canvas, 60″ × 60″*

special about these stones. But what is also fascinating is the fact that it appears all right to ask questions about such a visual reminder. Not everyone apparently would know what these stones meant. Those who were not there when they crossed the river Jordan with dry feet would not know. So someone has to explain the work of art called "the stones." Today, both artists and communities get upset when they do not "get" it, when someone has to explain what this image means or what that color represents in the sanctuary. But according to the Bible, it is all right to ask questions. As a matter of fact, asking questions is encouraged so that the story of what happened that day could be retold. It presented an opportunity to testify, to witness about what God had done. So we should recognize God's participation in everything, for the very materials we use, as I said earlier, reflect God's involvement.

But how do we make meaningful new reminders for ourselves and for our church communities? We must begin by recognizing that we have visual reminders, personal and communal ones, all around us: from family albums to high school yearbooks, from wedding texts to wedding rings. My parents had their wedding text hanging in their bedroom. The image of the words was a meaningful reminder for them of that event. For some reason we have become too sophisticated for that sort of thing. But it seems to me that there is much available today that is strange and shallow, from posters to coasters, from plaques to bumper stickers — and none of them challenges us to adore, to worship, to meditate or deepen our relationship, or to affirm our commitment.

Do you remember my curiosity about the twelve stones and how they were arranged? What made them conspicuous? Those are art questions, because they have to do with what we see with our eyes, not with our souls. I also hinted at this issue when I suggested that the very materials an artist uses have God-given power. Throughout Christian history, the visual arts have been employed to teach or convey the doctrines of the church. Like the biblical examples above, if you knew the codes, you could discover the meaning; if you knew the doctrine, you could connect the image to a complex series of understandings. Many of the visual traditions are intertwined with the oral traditions of the earlier histories. It is fascinating to follow the Gothic period, for example, and see the exchange between the artists and the theologians. Artists were commissioned but were very much directed by the theologians. When the theologians saw the visual form of what they had been directing, they responded and elaborated theologically. In the early Gothic period we see Christ portrayed as a judge, enthroned on the rainbow. Later Christ is the preacher and teacher, and in the late Gothic period he is the Christ who suffered and died on the cross. We can also explore the images of the Virgin Mary and see her change from the Queen of Heaven to the lowly maiden who gave birth to the Christ child.

There is, however, an inherent problem with the creation of visual reminders. Once the viewer "gets" the meaning, the visual becomes secondary; the original meaning is absorbed. The work becomes a kind of empty vessel for an intellectual concept; its emotional impact becomes predictable, and the image becomes a visual cliché. For artists, this becomes a special challenge: to take the symbol beyond the one level of meaning and endow it with additional levels: connecting, for example, cultural, theological, and historical elements to each other, intertwining them in a new set of relationships. This will make the image complex, and unique to a given culture. Each culture needs to discover its own visual reminders as it develops special interests and values. It is not enough to reclaim the old symbols; we need to invent new ones, images and reminders that will speak to us in our own day and reflect the way we live in this culture. But the image itself has to be visually attractive to begin functioning as art.

Besides the tradition of symbols, there is a tradition that has a narrative emphasis. From the pre-Christian era to our own time, there have been countless works that tell stories, biblical or otherwise, from a

Away with Him . . . ,
*1966, white ground
aquatint, 14″ × 15″*

particular perspective. Some would say that these works are a form of propaganda, that they represent only one point of view and can be interpreted only one way. Sometimes our modern ability to reproduce things has led to a deflation of the original work. The beautiful drawing made by Albrecht Dürer of the praying hands of his brother, for example, has lost its original power and impact. It has spawned bad imitations that have cheapened, if not demolished, the original intent. The mystery and struggle of Leonardo da Vinci to create the image of the Last Supper is no longer apparent, due to a spate of reproductions, many in the form of tasteless objects, from cups to platters, from hangings to doormats. A distinction must be made between decoration and art. Decoration done in a spirit of fun and joy can add a festive touch to any occasion or event. But that is quite different from what we have discussed art to be thus far. Art, whether it delights or angers us, touches us deeply within ourselves, challenges us to testify, and invites us to ponder. Decoration serves a specific occasion, whereas art transcends the narrow boundaries of any occasion.

The artist's struggle to create meaningful images and forms that speak to the issues of our day does not always make us feel comfortable. The Christian artist has a special task, in my view, to be prophetic in what he or she does. Some do that more successfully than others. When the artist challenges our values, chides us for our cultural laziness, and questions our lack of involvement in our immediate communities, we feel uncomfortable. When the artist behaves like a prophet of doom, we want to condemn his efforts as bizarre and strange, for we do not know how to respond when the artist confronts us through his images. Works of art that make us feel exposed and vulnerable may threaten our aesthetic ideals. But we must not condemn the work or the person for being prophetic. Neither must we condemn the artist who wants to function as a priest among us, nor reject the artist who wants to paint images that reveal the glory of our Lord and king.

The Artist and the Christian Community

As a church member I have been involved in the worship environment of our congregation. I have been an advisor to the Worship Institute and the Christian Reformed Church publication *Reformed Worship.* I have also participated in other art activities, such as speaking engagements, workshops, exhibitions, and competitions, organized by different congregations. Congregations can be creatively involved in the arts. There are a number of congregations, for example, that have set aside a space in the church for local Christian artists to display their work and to discuss their work with church members. Others have held annual juried art competitions, as the Peace Lutheran Church in Sparta, Michigan, did some forty years ago. Some of them have designated funds to purchase works from these competitions and have thus begun to collect the more meaningful works submitted in these competitions. Others have begun an Art Fund for the purpose of collecting works of art for the church building. Christian art organizations in many cities have begun to collect slides of the works of Christian artists in order to make the work of the living Christian masters available to the Christian community. More and more church publications are using the works of contemporary artists to enhance their productions. Such efforts, however, often concentrate on the biblical stories and events; other art forms created by Christian artists, such as landscape and cityscape paintings, are sometimes excluded from consideration.

So far I have avoided the use of the term "Christian art." I have carefully used the term "Christian artists" instead. What Christian artists make some would like to call Christian art. The problem is, when the Christian artist makes a fancy chair, does it become a Christian chair? Does everything the Christian artist makes automatically become Christian art? Or do we mean something else, like when the artist makes a biblical illustration?

A recent publication by Eric Newton and William Neil, called *2000 Years of Christian Art,* makes this claim. The authors define Christian art as being

Afterwards, *1986, oil on canvas, 66″ × 84″*

"an art that has no other preoccupation than the supernatural, the nature of man's relationship with God."

> But from the moment when God sent his only begotten Son to dwell on earth, born of a mortal woman, to preach, to perform miracles, to suffer death at the hands of the Jews, and to be resurrected, the situation for the artists changed, for a new religion contained within itself the fact of the invisible made visible, the Deity made human, the supernatural made physically manifest. (18)

To Newton and Neil, the Christmas event becomes the deciding moment for the arts, for it is a time when the "Word became flesh and dwelled among us." We saw and "beheld his glory." Nothing after that is the same, for all creation is his. All that we see around us belongs to the King. When we page through the book, however, we discover that it is filled with all kinds of works of art. But they are works of art that either express a theological concept or record a biblical event. Not by definition but by selection the authors have confused Christian art with Christian subject matter. But in my opinion, Christian subject matter does not make it Christian art. What if the artist was an atheist? A non-believer who needed some money to support his drug habit? Would we call that work Christian art? Is there, then, a way to make art in a Christian manner? I believe the icons of the Orthodox Church come very close. Icons are special images, and the act of making an icon is an act of prayer; the image is meant to call attention to our need for prayer. Icons should not call attention to themselves. The icon of a crucifix, for example, should not have excellencies or subtleties that would distract from calling us to prayer. Icons are therefore not intended to be visual explorations. They are reflective of a visual as well as a religious tradition.

Some Christian artists like myself have become involved in liturgical art. Liturgical art can assist the Christian community in special ways, like altering the worship environment, making meaningful vessels for the communion celebration, or designing pulpit furniture that is more than functional. Such art works can rightfully be called liturgical art as well as Christian art because of the way they are peculiarly meaningful to the Christian community. It is within the context of the community that art becomes Christian. There is thus a place within the Christian community for liturgical art. It is also fitting that this same community develops an appreciation for biblical narrative painting.

But what do we do with all the other arts? When a Christian artist like myself makes a large landscape awesome in its use of space, mysterious in its atmosphere, and inspiring in its use of light — is it just a landscape? And because it is a landscape, can it not be Christian art? A Jewish New York critic who had been asked to select the exhibition at the Biennial Conference of the Christian in the Visual Arts (CIVA) was confronted by one of the landscapes I had entered in the competition. His reply at first was: "No, a landscape does not belong in a Christian art competition, but upon seeing this work, I have decided that it should be included. This artist made us aware of God's marvelous creation." Later that same work received top honors in another Christian art competition.

All of this illustrates that the term "Christian art" is confusing and even misleading, especially when we attempt to define it. My difficulty comes from the object called "art," be it a painting, drawing, pulpit, or even a Bible. Can such an object be transformed into a "Christian" object? I think not. It may be special; it may even have a special place within the worship space as a reminder of some major theological concept. But it does not become a Christian object. I believe there are dedicated Christian artists who respond Christianly to God's world and word. They are artists whose works will reveal and retell, will enable us to confess and glorify the Lord. But above all, the works will invite us to see.

Seeing requires observing. When we look, what do we see? So often we look because we do not want to stumble. We use our eyes to prevent us from falling down a step or from tripping on uneven pavement. As an artist

I have learned to look by drawing. Drawing an object is a wonderful way to really see it. Writing down what you see is another way of concentrating on what is in front of you. Seeing can be describing for some. By looking we become aware. The British author and critic John Ruskin recognized this when he said that the paintings of Joseph Turner alerted him to the color of the sky. I can personally testify that my own cloud paintings have made people aware of the sky. Art therefore can increase our awareness. Many individuals have told me that they saw "my clouds." Some even sent me their photographs to prove it. But did they see what I saw? Did they get the deeper meaning expressed by Nicholas Wolterstorff in the introduction to the catalog *Twenty-Five Years as an American Artist*?: ". . . the nature projected does not diminish but exalts. And it is not a nature alien to us but a nature in which we are at home . . . these are paintings of shalom. We are neither nature's aggressive conquerors nor nature's submissive moles but participants in the grandeur of nature . . . [he] celebrates God's majesty and glory in the world of fields and clouds and space" (7-8).

Art has many levels. Some levels we can analyze by applying the elements and principles of design. The visual elements of art are line, shape, value, texture, and color. These are what I call the non-debatable, for it is seldom asked: Is that a line, or is that a shape, or does this work have color? What the line is doing there is another matter, and that is why we talk about the principles of design, sometimes called the organizational components. The best way for me to remember them is to place them across from the elements: line and direction (sometimes called movement), shape and variation (which can include dominance and scale), texture and repetition, value and contrast, color and harmony. The elements and the principles are there to help us discuss and analyze how a work is constructed so that we can begin to understand the visual components, recognizing at the same time that there are many other factors at work when we view a work of art.

A good work of art will have many levels. The more levels, the greater our interest and our appreciation of a given work. For example: there is

Dieric Bouts, Last Supper Altarpiece, *1464 – 67, oil on panel, 35″ × 28″ each wing (Church of St. Peter, Louvain)*

often a historic context for a given work, and sometimes definite meanings were recommended by people who commissioned the work. In a publication by Wolfgang Stechow, there is a wonderful document that records in detail what Dieric Bouts was ordered to include in his painting of the Last Supper:

> In this altarpiece there shall be presented on the center panel the Supper of our Beloved Lord with his Twelve Apostles, and on each of the inner wings two presentations from the Old Testament: (1) the Heavenly Bread, (2) Melchizedek, (3) Elijah, (4) the Eating of the Paschal Lamb as described in the Old Covenant. . . . And the aforementioned Master Dieric has contracted to make this altarpiece to the best of his ability, to spare neither labor or time, but to do his utmost to demonstrate in it the art which God has bestowed on him, in such order and truth as the Reverend Masters Jan Vaernacker and Gillis Bailuwel, Professors of Theology, shall prescribe to him with regards to the aforementioned subjects. (11)

If we can find out what gave impetus to the work, we may gain some appreciation for the context. Identifying the subject is a good thing as long as we do not stop at that point, for the manner in which the subject is presented is crucial to our experience of the work. That is what the artist calls the content; the manner in which a subject is presented will show how the artist thought about the subject. How does the work fit with the idea that is being portrayed? The more works we see and study in this way, the better our sense will be about what is right and what is fitting. The notion of fittingness is familiar to us. We know when to dress up for an official occasion, such as a wedding, because we want to fit in with the rest. We know to dress casually if we are attending a picnic, because again we want to fit in. Artists are sometimes asked if they have a painting in certain colors so that it will fit above the sofa or the piano. That is one way to think about fittingness, of course. Another way is less pragmatic and more reflective: How does it fit with me as a Christian? How does it fit with my soul?

The Grace Christian Reformed Church Symbol, 1968

"Fittingness" is an interesting word. It is the kind of word philosophers of aesthetics, like Nicholas Wolterstorff, like to use. In his book *Art in Action*, Wolterstorff talks about the artist and fittingness in great detail. He states, "every artist . . . is a worker in fittingness" (96). I would like to explore two different kinds of fittingness. First, fittingness may mean that two different things, like a concept and an image, need to fit together. The second meaning refers to the fittingness *within* a visual image. Let us look at the Grace Church symbol and explore the different ideas that may fit. The Grace Church symbol includes a crown of thorns — a reminder of the suffering, atonement, sacrifice, humiliation, and salvation offered through grace by Christ Jesus. It also has a triangle — a reminder of the triune God, Father, Son, Holy Spirit, and the triune plan of salvation. Within the dark triangle there is the image of a dove coming down as the Spirit comes down to us, making us aware, introducing us to Christ. All of this suggests the first fittingness, that of image and idea. The symbol, however, also has visual fittingness. The first thing we see are the sharp thorns of the red crown, and these sharp thorns are echoed by the corners of the triangle. These sharp elements reflect the concept of suffering, but they also relate the various parts to each other, for the shape of the dove repeats other shapes found in the crown of thorns. All of the shapes and lines are intertwined interestingly with each other, using repetition to unify, yet maintaining a great sense of variety. In this manner the symbols become a single visual unit.

The theological concepts and ideas incorporated into the Grace Church symbol fit the overall concept of grace. They also reflect a visual unity within its design. These two different kinds of fittingness can also be applied to the worship space and the worship services planned for that space.

The Artist and the Church

Over the past thirty years I have served the church in several ways. I have served as a deacon, as an elder, as a Sunday School teacher, as Vice-President of Council and of the elders; but the most satisfying service for me was as a member of the Worship Committee and as the Worship Environmentalist at Grace Christian Reformed Church in Grand Rapids. This should not come as a surprise, for I have already discussed the idea of service and community. The church is one very important community to me.

The Reformed tradition is supposedly known for its austere, clean, and simple worship environment. Reformed churches eliminated all the stuff that distracted from the simple, direct worship of God. But even when we have a simple worship environment (which seldom seems to be the case nowadays), we are still confronted with the issue of how particular elements of worship fit together. Artists often raise questions about priorities, questions about commitment, relationships, and order. When we ask questions about fittingness, we are asking the kinds of questions with which artists struggle. Artists are trained to create order — visual order. They are skilled in organizing visual objects within a certain space.

Installation, "Ordinary Times," Grace Christian Reformed Church, Grand Rapids, Michigan, 1980s

The question we raised some thirty, thirty-five years ago was whether we should introduce more variety into our public worship services. Would it be appropriate to recognize that the period of Advent, which is filled with anticipation of the coming of the Lord, is different from the period of Lent, which is filled with the pain and suffering of that same Lord? Should our worship environment reflect these differences so that we are challenged to meditate and encouraged to anticipate? At Grace Church we defined the liturgical space within the sanctuary with long, narrow, colored banners; a wide banner was used behind the pulpit, and smaller, previously designed banners were hung in front of this wider banner. Color began to dominate the space, and when we repeated this installation in red for Pentecost and in blue-purple for the season of Advent, we discovered the impact that color can have on a space. We then began to explore other ways that went beyond the initial banners. We found that the introduction of color, lots of it, greatly enhanced the worship environment.

The church in its history has used the liturgical colors for centuries, and many churches are now following the liturgical year, if not the liturgical lexicon, and have introduced the liturgical color scheme: Advent, purple or blue-purple; Christmas and all holidays, white, including Epiphany, Easter, and Ascension; Pentecost is red. Lent is also purple but more a red-purple. In many churches only the cloth on the Lord's Table and the pulpit is changed with the seasons. Such minor adjustments to our worship space have little or no impact on the worshiper.

Images, when they are used in the worship space, have to fit; they have to fit the season and the particular emphasis a minister or a worship committee has established for that particular year or part of the year. A good reminder at this point is the Joshua story. For those Israelites who did not cross the dry riverbed of the Jordan, not everything was clear; they had to be told. If something is unclear or questionable before the public worship service, will it be clear afterwards because we were part of the service?

Installation, Grace Christian Reformed Church, for Good Friday Service, 1980s (left)

Installation, Grace Christian Reformed Church, for Easter Sunday Service, 1980s (right)

That would be applying the principle we discovered in Joshua. At Grace Church we seldom print an explanation in the bulletin. Sometimes, during or before his sermon, the minister calls attention to any modifications in the imagery or ambience, thus providing insight and understanding.

Creating images for worship can be a personal act of worship. It does not always work out perfectly, especially when you do it for the first time. There is still much to learn, much to explore. I have gradually learned not to be too discouraged, or defend too vigorously what I have done. Working with a worship committee helps; sometimes the committee actually sides with the artist.

As a last example of how we can serve the church, I would like to describe the Graafschap Project. The Graafschap Project was another history project. After I had given an initial lecture to the Graafschap Church Historical Committee, we proceeded with a contract to define the various steps. This was an active committee that wanted to be involved in the process, and the work itself was a delight to create. It included some sixty or more portraits of people who had belonged to the congregation, and a number of events, with an emphasis on preaching and the celebration of the sacraments. The theme for the celebration was "From Generation to Generation." The painting, 48″ × 60″, is now displayed in the history room at the church. Serving the church in this way was deeply satisfying and significant for me — a returning of art to the community.

In conclusion: the Christian artist and the Christian community need to find ways in which to respect and appreciate each other. The community should be open to new ways and new approaches, so that artists have the freedom to use their talents in the service of that community. We need to recognize that we need each other. The artists among us need the support of the Christian community, and the Christian community needs the contributions of the artists. In an age when we are surrounded by trivial images, we need the insights and sensibilities of real artists to regain our sense of judgment and learn again to discern what is good and noble.

THIS DO IN REMEMBRANCE OF ME

From Generation to Generation: 150 Years of Graafschap Christian Reformed Church, 1997, oil on canvas, 48″ × 60″

The Artist and the Community

A number of years ago Alexander Calder, an internationally known American sculptor famous for inventing mobiles, was commissioned to make a piece for the Grand Rapids city plaza. The city had just opened a new City Hall and County Building. Both new structures stood next to each other, surrounded by a major plaza. The resulting sculpture, "La Grand Vitesse" (The Great Swiftness), was installed in front on the city/county plaza. It was a controversial stabile made of steel and painted a bright red, and the public debate it aroused, much of it covered by the media, was exhaustive and heated. However, the "Calder," as it has become commonly known, exerted a stabilizing influence on the city, and now, after a number of years, it has become the symbol of the city's revitalization. The "Calder" became a focal point; nowadays when you look around, images of that wonderful red stabile can be found on city street signs, garbage trucks, and stationery. Even the water bill I receive in the mail has the image of the "Calder" on it. A work of art that started out controversially has become the symbol for the city of Grand Rapids. A work of art acquired the power to unite a floundering city. Clearly, art has played a major role in our local community.

I have already described the Vietnam Veterans Memorial and the healing power it has provided to our nation. As a result of this monument, we are now actively searching for a monument that will commemorate World War II. These are but two examples in which public art has functioned for our city and our country. The city of Grand Rapids has in fact become a city of public sculpture: from the "Calder" to the citywide exhibition "Sculpture Off the Pedestal," to the twenty-seven-foot-high bronze horse made from drawings by Leonardo da Vinci. This latest work, in the Frederik Meijer Gardens, shows that the tradition of sculpture is alive and well in our city.

The Artist in Academe

As a faculty member of Calvin College, I have served as the Artist in Residence twice. The college also provided me with other opportunities to serve and participate in different kinds of communities. As Director of "Connections: A Baroque Festival Year," it was my responsibility to connect the various academic communities with the larger communities within western Michigan. As Director of the Multicultural Year, it was my responsibility to connect with various minority groups and agencies. The ideal of connecting art to the community has motivated my commitment in these various endeavors. This was especially true when I served as Director of Exhibitions for Calvin College. Serving on the board of the Art Museum, the Municipal Arts Advisory Committee, the Grand Rapids Arts Council, and on advisory panels of the Michigan Council for the Arts also connected me to different segments of our society as an artist. I have learned from each of these activities that the artist must participate in his or her respective community to prepare the soil in which art can flourish. As makers of art, we should begin the dialogue if we are to have a meaningful relationship with our communities. For too long, artists and their communities have been isolated and separated from each other. Since my retirement, I have become involved with the Grand Rapids Art Museum as a volunteer in Visitor Services and as a Docent. I have also served on the Grand Rapids Art Museum Volunteer Association Board and on the Board of Trustees. It is a good place for me to remain active and share what I have learned these past few years.

The Artist and the Museum

The art museum is a great place, for it preserves the work of the old masters. It is a place where works are looked after and the latest techniques of conservation and preservation are applied to various works of art and design. It is also a place where we can study the works of the past and discover relationships and connections among these works when they are mounted in various exhibitions. Such showings are sometimes surprising, for there is no distinction made between the works made for small private homes and those created for large worship spaces. The altar and the cabinet pieces live together in the exhibition hall. Sometimes a museum succeeds in creating a fitting environment in which the original context is to some extent regained. Though the museum is not a place of worship, it is nonetheless a good place to contemplate and reflect on works of art.

The museum is a showplace for both living and old masters. For many art museums, the tension between the living masters and their demands and the old masters of previous years is an unresolved issue. Few, if any, of the living masters get solo exhibitions. Most artists need to be satisfied with local or regional commercial galleries. Educational galleries offer a greater degree of opportunity.

The Artist and the Schools

In previous chapters I discussed my limited exposure to art in the elementary Christian school I attended. Large reproductions of historical events made a lasting impression upon me as a child. The elementary school should be a place where art is much in evidence; historical, religious, and biblical images as well as landscapes, clowns, and other forms of expression should decorate the halls and classrooms. With today's technology it is relatively easy to collect a large number of reproductions, so that art of all kinds can be displayed. When I visit schools, it always strikes me how bare the halls are and how cluttered the classrooms. Sometimes there is an attempt to introduce color here and there. Occasionally it works, but such attempts at decorating are a far cry from the meaningful images of the art world. How students can function quietly and calmly in a classroom environment that visually screams at me remains a mystery to me. School should be a place where creativity is encouraged and nurtured across the curriculum — not just in the art room, if there is one, but in every classroom, laboratory, and library.

Creativity can be found in all human activities and is not a special gift reserved for artists only. Artists do not have a corner on inventiveness and innovation, nor do I believe that they have greater problem-solving ability.

Everyone can be creative in some way. Every time a new solution is found to a problem — technical, personal, or communal — someone has been creative. The engineer who builds a bridge needs to employ creativity and solid engineering to get us across the river safely and in style. The person who can bring a community together needs to be creatively involved in that community. The same is true for any personal relationship. In other words, creative behavior will help you live better. As a Christian community, we need to recognize that "creativity is God's gift to us." Using your creativity is your gift back to God.

Creative behavior is therefore a desirable activity that we need to encourage in ourselves as well as in others. We will begin to see more, hear more, and enjoy more when we do. A deepening of our awareness will bring us to a point where we will see and hear things that others are unaware of. By sharing our awareness with others, we will call them to attention and reveal to them what they are missing. This task in some sense is given to believers and non-believers alike. The Christian believer may be especially challenged to testify more intensely to the power and grandeur of our God, the Creator and Redeemer, the one who upholds the universe. But the unbeliever may unknowingly provide the same testimony.

Conclusion

Two phrases come to mind for a conclusion. Both are Latin phrases that you will occasionally find on Dutch homes. The first is a phrase that was used extensively in the nineteenth century by the followers of Abraham Kuyper: "soli deo gloria." It summarized their goals and lifestyles: to God alone be the glory. In this book I have repeatedly stated that God is first. Someone recently pointed out to me that prayer is not asking, but answering. Prayer is a response to what God has already done in Christ. Our lives as Christians and our lives as artists should be like that, responses to what God has done. Being an artist is not an easy life, for we are forever sticking our neck out about a whole bunch of issues. But in response to what Jesus did, we can live lives filled with joy and thanksgiving. The little frustrations about our inability to make good stuff, the lack of recognition, the rejection slip from a competition, the lackluster reception, must all be placed in that larger perspective of the ultimate concern: Christ's love for us.

The other phrase is a marvelous follow-up, for it encourages us to work and to keep our work in perspective: "ora et labora" — pray and work. Prayer is not going to complete our artworks; we need to work at that ourselves. But we also need to keep in perspective why we work: we are responding in work and in prayer to our God, the Creator of us all.

Allen, Pat B. *Art Is a Way of Knowing.* Boston & London: Shambhala, 1995.

Bernard, Bruce. *De Bijbel in de Schilderkunst.* Kampen, the Netherlands: Kok; Leuven, Belgium: Davidsfonds, 1984.

Chinn, Nancy. *Spaces for Spirit: Adorning the Church.* Chicago: Archdiocese of Chicago, Liturgy Training Publication, 1998.

Dewey, John. *Art as Experience.* New York: Capricorn Books, 1958.

De Leeuw, Ronald. *The Letters of Vincent van Gogh.* London: Penguin Books, 1997.

Edwards, Betty. *Drawing on the Right Side of the Brain.* Los Angeles: Jeremy Tarcher, 1979.

Exhibition Catalog: *Chris Stoffel Overvoorde: Twenty-Five Years as an American Artist.* Calvin College Art Department. Grand Rapids: Calvin College, 1986.

Exhibition Catalog: *PRAIRIEVISION.* Calvin College Art Department. Grand Rapids: Calvin College, 1994.

Exhibition Catalog: *Kunstfeest: Diversity.* Calvin College Art Department. Grand Rapids: Calvin College, 1997.

Flack, Audrey. *Art and Soul: Notes on Creating.* New York: E. P. Dutton, 1986.

Hoffman, Donald. *Lifelong Learning and the Visual Arts.* New York: National Endowment for the Arts, 1980.

Hughes, Robert. *Nothing If Not Critical.* New York: Penguin Books, 1987.

Jacobs, Edwin, et al. *J. H. Weissenbruch, 1824-1903*. Den Haag, the Netherlands: Museum Jan Cunen & Gemeente Museum Den Haag, Exhibition Catalog, 1999.

Lockerbie, Bruce. *The Liberating Word: Art and the Mystery of the Gospel*. Grand Rapids: Eerdmans, 1974.

Newton, Eric, and William Neil. *2000 Years of Christian Art*. New York: Harper & Row, 1966.

Overvoorde, Chris Stoffel, and Ann Saigeon. *Stories of Faith: Fifteen Heroes of Calvin College and the Christian Reformed Church*. Grand Rapids: Calvin College, 1993.

Ryken, Leland, et al. *The Christian Imagination: Essays on Literature and the Arts*. Grand Rapids: Baker, 1981.

Seerveld, Calvin. *Rainbows for the Fallen World*. Toronto: Tuppence Press, 1980.

Stechow, Wolfgang. *Northern Renaissance Art, 1400-1600*. Englewood Cliffs, N.J.: Prentice-Hall, 1996.

Thompson, Thomas, et al. *The One in the Many: Christian Identity in a Multicultural World*. New York, Lanham, Md., and Oxford: Calvin Center Series and University Press of America, 1998.

Tobias, Cynthia Ulrich. *The Way We Work*. Colorado Springs: Focus on the Family Publishing, 1995.

————. *The Way They Learn*. Colorado Springs: Focus on the Family Publishing, 1994.

Wolterstorff, Nicholas. *Art in Action: Towards a Christian Aesthetics*. Grand Rapids: Eerdmans, 1980.

This Agreement made in duplicate _____ (date) between

> THE REDEEMER COLLEGE ART GALLERY
> Redeemer Reformed Christian College
> 777 Highway 53 East, Ancaster, Ontario
> (hereinafter called the "Gallery") OF THE FIRST PART

and: CHRIS STOFFEL OVERVOORDE
2317 DeLange Dr. SE
Grand Rapids, Michigan
(hereinafter called the "Artist") OF THE SECOND PART

1. EXHIBIT. The Gallery will present a solo exhibition of works by the Artist as per schedule and agreed to by both parties from (date) _____ to (date) _____.

2. GALLERY. The works will be exhibited in that part of the Gallery space commonly referred to as "the Gallery," that is, the second floor of the north wing of the Academic Building.

3. WORKS. The Gallery can request that any work or works which, in the exclusive opinion of the College, the College deems to be at variance with the College's Mission Statement, Institutional Purpose, Statement of Basic Principles, be removed from the body of works proposed to constitute the exhibition, or, in case such works constitute a substantial part of the exhibition, that the

exhibition be cancelled, at the time of the final selection for the exhibition, with no penalty to the College.

4. PROGRAM. The Artist will provide biographical information, a list of works with titles, medium, and support, size (height precedes width precedes depth), and valuation for insurance purposes to the Gallery not less than sixty days prior to the opening of the exhibition.

5. ANNOUNCEMENT. The Gallery will arrange announcements of the exhibition, at its expense, in its usual publications and as part of its usual advertising in the media.

6. OPENING. The Gallery will sponsor an event such as an official opening, or a "meet the artist" session during the exhibition, and will invite up to 100 persons as indicated by the Artist, as well as others who may be invited through the Gallery's publicity program.

7. The Artist agrees to be present with the works on the official opening, or another date as may be required.

8. HANGING. The Gallery will be responsible for hanging and displaying the works, in consultation with the Artist.

9. EXHIBITION FEE. The gallery will pay an exhibition fee of _____ to the Artist for the exhibition, within thirty days after the closing of the exhibition. This fee gives the right to the Gallery to make photographs, or other images, of the works for a handlist/catalogue/information sheet, or other publicity purposes associated with the exhibition.

10. CANCELLATION. In the event that the Gallery cancels the exhibition, it will pay liquidation fees to the Artist according to the following schedule of written notice being mailed:

More than ninety days notice	no fee
Ninety to thirty days notice	$50.00
Less than thirty days notice	full exhibition fee

11. INCAPACITY. In the event that the Artist is not able to provide the works to be exhibited on the dates agreed to, thereby causing the exhibition to be cancelled, the Artist will pay liquidation fees to the Gallery according to the following schedule:

more than ninety days notice	no fee
ninety to thirty days notice	$50.00
less than thirty days notice	full exhibition fee

12. READY WORKS. The Artist will be responsible for having the works ready for exhibition prior to (date) _____. All works are to be in a condition suitable for display (including matting and framing).

13. SHIPPING. The cost of shipping the works from the Artist to the Gallery and returning them to the Artist (at the same location from which they were picked up) is the responsibility of the Gallery. The Gallery will return to the Artist or the Artist's agent all works except any which may have been purchased by the Gallery, within fifteen days of the last day of the exhibition. The method of shipping will be _____.

14. INSURANCE. The Gallery shall be responsible for insuring the works during transit to the Gallery, while on exhibition, and while in transit to the Artist after the close of the exhibition.

15. REPRODUCTION. The Gallery will not permit reproduction of the works for the purpose of sale, rental, loan, or distribution of any kind except as provided herein.

16. CO-SPONSOR. In the circumstances of an exhibition to be sponsored jointly by the Gallery and another mutual party, the engagement of the co-sponsor is with the full knowledge and mutual consent of the Artist and the Gallery.

17. PREVENTION. In the event that any part of this agreement on the part of the Artist or the Gallery shall be prevented by an Act of God, physical disability, the acts of regulations or duly constituted authorities, strike, civic tumult, war, epidemic, interruption or delay of transportation services, or other cause beyond their control, each shall be relieved of their obligations hereunder during the period such prevention exists. It is understood and agreed that there shall be no claim for damages by either part of the agreement.

18. AMENDMENTS. All amendments and modifications to this agreement shall be with the written consent of both parties.

In witness thereof, the parties have caused this agreement to be executed:

Signed by the Artist in the presence of

_____   _____
Witness   Signature of Artist

_____   _____
Printed name of Witness   Printed name of Artist

_____
Date

Signed by the Gallery in the presence of

_____   _____
Witness   Signature of President

_____   _____
Printed name of Witness   Printed name of President

_____
Date

Appendix C: Art Gallery Contract

Standard Art Consignment Agreement

The Artist (name, address, and telephone number)

____

____

____

____

The Gallery (name, address, and telephone number)

____

____

____

____

hereby enter into the following Agreement:

1. AGENCY PURPOSES. The Artist appoints the Gallery as agent for the works of art ("the Artworks") consigned under this agreement, for the purpose of exhibition and sale. The Gallery shall not permit the Artworks to be used for any other purposes without the written consent of the Artist.

2. CONSIGNMENT. The Artist hereby consigns to the gallery, and the Gallery accepts on consignment, those Artworks listed on the attached Inventory Sheet which is part of this agreement. Additional Inventory Sheets may be incorporated into this agreement at such

time as both parties agree to the consignment of other works of art. All Inventory Sheets shall be signed by the Artist and the Gallery.

3. Warranty. The Artist hereby warrants that he/she created and possesses unencumbered titles to the Artworks, and that their descriptions are true and accurate.

4. Duration of Consignment. The Artist and the Gallery agree that the initial term of the consignment for the Artworks is to be _____ (months), and that the Artist does not intend to request their return before the end of this term. Thereafter, consignment shall continue until the Artist requests the return of any or all of the Artworks, with which request the other party shall comply promptly.

5. Transportation Responsibilities. Packing and shipping charges, insurance costs, other handling expenses, and risk of loss or damage incurred in the delivery of the Artworks from the Artist to the Gallery, and in their return to the Artist, shall be the responsibility of the _____ (specify Gallery or Artist).

6. Responsibility for Loss or Damage: Insurance Coverage. The Gallery shall be responsible for the safekeeping of all consigned Artworks while they are in its custody. The Gallery shall be strictly liable to the Artist for their loss or damage (except for damage resulting from flaws inherent in the Artworks), to the full amount the Artist would have received from the Gallery if the Artworks had been sold. The Gallery shall provide the Artist with all relevant information about its insurance coverage for the Artworks if the Artist requests this information.

7. Fiduciary Responsibilities. Title to each of the Artworks remains with the Artist until the Artist has been paid the full amount owed him or her for the Artworks; title then passes directly to the

purchaser. All proceeds from the sale of the Artworks shall be held in trust for the Artist. The Gallery shall pay all amounts due the Artist before any proceeds of sales can be made available to creditors of the Gallery.

8. NOTICE OF CONSIGNMENT. The Gallery shall give notice, by means of a clear and conspicuous sign in full public view, that certain works of art are being sold subject to a contract of consignment.

9. REMOVAL FROM GALLERY. The Gallery shall not lend out, remove from the premises, or sell on approval any of the Artworks, without first obtaining written permission of the Artist.

10. PRICING, GALLERY'S COMMISSION, TERMS OF PAYMENT. The Gallery shall sell the Artworks only at the Retail Price specified on the Inventory Sheet. The Gallery and the Artist agree that the Gallery's commission is to be _____% of the Retail Price of the Artwork. Any change in the Retail Price, or in the Gallery's commission, must be agreed to in advance by the Artist and the Gallery. Payment to the Artist shall be made by the Gallery within _____ days after the date of sale of any of the Artworks. The Gallery assumes full risk for the failure to pay on the part of any purchaser to whom it has sold an Artwork.

11. PROMOTION. The Gallery shall use its best efforts to promote the sale of the Artworks. The Gallery agrees to provide adequate display of the Artworks, and to undertake other promotional activities on the Artist's behalf, as follows: _____ _____. The Gallery and the Artist shall agree in advance on the division of artistic control and financial responsibility for expenses incurred in the Gallery's exhibitions and other promotional activities undertaken on the Artist's behalf.

12. REPRODUCTION. The Artist reserves all rights to the reproduction of the Artworks except as noted in writing to the contrary. The Gallery may arrange to have the Artworks photographed to publicize and promote the Artworks through means to be agreed to by both parties. In every instance of such use, the Artist shall be acknowledged as the creator and copyright owner of the Artwork. The Gallery shall include on each bill of sale of any Artwork the following legend: "All rights reserved to reproduction of the work(s) of art identified herein are retained by the artist."

13. ACCOUNTING. A statement of accounts for all sales of the Artworks shall be furnished by the Gallery to the Artist on a regular basis, in a form agreed to by both parties, as follows _____ (specify frequency and manner of accounting). The Artist shall have the right to inventory his or her Artworks in the Gallery and to inspect any books and records pertaining to sales of the Artworks.

14. ADDITIONAL PROVISIONS:

· EXCLUSIVITY. The Artist agrees that he/she will not market Artworks in other galleries within a _____ mile radius of said Gallery _____. The Gallery is entitled to all commissions derived from Artworks sold within the aforementioned radius excluding works that are in the Artist's Studio or Home. Such Artworks will remain available to designers and friends. No commission will be paid for the Artworks that have not been in the Gallery.

· Annual creative output — Artworks per month/ year

_____.

· Artist responsible for the appropriate framing of the Artworks (if applicable)

· Artist will provide Gallery with an "Artist's Statement" and a current resume.

15. TERMINATION OF AGREEMENT. Notwithstanding any other provision of this Agreement, this Agreement may be terminated at any time by either the Gallery or the Artist, by means of written notification of termination from either party to the other. In the event of the Artist's death, the estate of the Artist shall have the right to terminate the Agreement. Within thirty days of the notification of termination, all accounts shall be settled and all unsold Artworks shall be returned by the Gallery.

16. PROCEDURES FOR MODIFICATION. Amendments to this agreement must be signed by both Artist and Gallery and attached to this Agreement. Both parties must initial any deletions made on this form and any additional provisions written onto it.

17. MISCELLANY. This Agreement represents the entire agreement between the Artist and the Gallery. If any part of this agreement is held to be illegal, void, or unenforceable for any reason, such holdings shall not affect the validity and enforceability of any other part. A waiver of any breach of the same provision of this Agreement shall not be construed as a continuing waver of other breaches of the same provisions or other provisions hereof. This Agreement shall not be assigned nor shall it inure to the benefit of the successors of the Gallery, whether by operation of law or otherwise, without the written consent of the Artist.

18. CHOICE OF LAW. This agreement shall be governed by the law of the State of Michigan.

_____   _____
Signature of Artist   Signature of authorized
                                                                 representative of the Gallery

LaGrave Avenue Christian Reformed Church

This is an agreement between Chris Stoffel Overvoorde, artist, and the Centennial Committee of the LaGrave Avenue Christian Reformed Church.

Chris Stoffel Overvoorde agrees to the following:

1. To paint nine (9) original paintings for the Centennial Committee. The paintings will be done in oil on canvas and will be in size two (2) feet by two (2) feet each.

2. Before proceeding with each painting, a layout (rough sketch) will be prepared to show what the finished product will contain. These layouts (rough sketches) will be presented to Keith Winn, representing the Centennial Committee, who must give approval before Chris Stoffel Overvoorde proceeds with the painting.

3. The nine (9) paintings will be completed by October 1, 1986.

4. It is estimated that each work will require 30-40 hours of painting, drawing and planning, at a fee of _____ per hour. This price does not include framing. An amount not to exceed $600.00 will be paid for supplies.

5. The cost figures will be reviewed after three (3) paintings have been completed.

The Centennial Committee agrees to the following:

1. To do the necessary fact finding and research work that Chris Stoffel Overvoorde determines is necessary for each painting.

2. To pay Chris Stoffel Overvoorde _____ an hour per painting as the paintings are completed.

3. To pay Chris Stoffel Overvoorde up to $600.00 for supplies needed to complete the paintings.

4. To pay for the cost of mounting and framing the paintings.

5. To have Keith Winn act for the committee in reviewing the proposed layouts (rough sketches) and giving Chris Stoffel Overvoorde approval to proceed with the paintings.

Agreed to on this 1st day of July, 1986

_____   _____
Artist signature   Committee Signature

Note: Whenever a concept could be presented with a color scheme and a rather extensive detailed drawing in the actual size of the painting, the committee would meet and approve the work. After the approval I would have some freedom to complete the work. It was understood that once the committee accepted the image we would not change it afterwards. I wanted to avoid being second-guessed by the committee after I had completed the work. It was a good process.